The Road To

Joy and Happiness

How To:

Develop Life-Changing Habits,

Change Negative Behaviors,

and

Create The Life You Want

Byron Pulsifer, Catherine Pulsifer

Also by Byron Pulsifer

The Road To Joy and Happiness How To: Develop Life-Changing Habits,
Change Negative Behaviors, and Create The Life You Want
The Confidence Guide: 27 Proven Ways To Build Your Self-Worth

Watch for more at https://pulsiferbooks.com.

Also by Catherine Pulsifer

Wings

Wings for Work: Learn How To Develop and Use The Three Key Qualities
That Successful People Have Mastered

Wings for Goals: How To Use Three Easy Steps to Change Your Life Forever!

Standalone

Millionaire's Key Habits for Success: Adopt Their Attitudes To Create The
Life You Want

Wings of Wisdom: Your Daily Guide to Benefit from Change, Profit from
Failure, and Design Your Own Destiny!

The Road To Joy and Happiness How To: Develop Life-Changing Habits,
Change Negative Behaviors, and Create The Life You Want

The Confidence Guide: 27 Proven Ways To Build Your Self-Worth

Watch for more at https://pulsiferbooks.com.

Table of Contents

LEGAL DISCLAIMER

INTRODUCTION

There is an age-old question that we are all familiar with and it is probably the reason you downloaded this book. And that question is, 'what is happiness'? However, the more important question is 'how do I attain happiness'?

So, what about joy in life?

Let's be clear. There is a difference between joy and happiness. The discussion will unfold to discuss both joy and happiness, where joy and happiness are not distant cousins. The question I will answer is, can we obtain happiness separate from seeking joy? Or is the pursuit of joy separate from experiencing happiness?

You would probably agree that joy and happiness are two concepts that everyone strives to attain. The difference between joy and happiness will become clear, and the inter-relationship between them, as you read on through the book.

But, for clarification, this is how I define joy and happiness.

❖ Happiness is a momentary (short-term) emotion, externally triggered, and a single flash in time with triggers such as events, things, location, or other people. We learn to savor each moment of happiness when it appears rather than allow it to pass us by unnoticed.

❖ Joy is more meaningful and profound (long-term) and cultivated from within. It is a sense of inner peace or contentment, despite the world's obstacles and uncertainty. It can provide stability in times of difficulty and help people move through and beyond current struggles.

Though both emotions are desirable, it is important to recognize the differences between them for the true attainment of either. I begin, therefore, with the assumption that joy and happiness are inseparable, meaning that without one, the other cannot fully be realized.

In a culture obsessed with material success where people can purchase a vast array of material objects that seem to promote a feeling of happiness, its effects are only short term.

———————

We often hear that having an optimistic outlook on life can aid in achieving a desirable state of being, that is a state of happiness. However, it is important to think beyond the idea that simply being positive will lead to happiness and consider how one's individual outlook, whether it be positive or negative, contributes to their quality of life.

In a practical sense, when someone looks at life through a pessimistic lens, they are likely to encounter more obstacles and adverse situations than those who view things from a more optimistic perspective.

However, this does not mean that optimism guarantees success and contentment; there are always going to be disappointments and difficulties, regardless of one's mindset. However, if someone approaches each situation with positivity rather than pessimism, then their chances of finding joy in the experience increases. Notice I didn't say 'finding happiness from the experience'; there are reasons that will become clear later.

Marcus A. Antoninus said, "the happiness of your life depends on the quality of your thoughts." If this is true, then we can achieve joy and happiness through the quality of our thoughts.

Other people would suggest that satisfaction with possessing enough money to house, clothe and feed themselves or their family is all that is needed to be happy. Is this all that is needed for joy and happiness?

Then there are types of people who know that life is a steady quest, and that nothing is ever achieved without effort? If this is so, it means that a person must work for it and not merely wish that it will be so. But, what does 'effort' mean? How much? How often?

Or, is happiness dependent on who defines it?

If this is the case, we would have many definitions based on several factors including income, health, friendships, relationships, marriage, children, artistic talent, enough food on the table, no legal problems, great businesses, academic credentials, and so on. Is there any end to the list?

Are any of these assumptions correct? Let's find out.

HISTORICAL PERSPECTIVES

———

The quest for joy and happiness is anything but a modern-day pursuit. The following historical perspectives are a small sampling of various views and definitions of happiness that have occurred throughout time and should not be construed as a complete historical review.

The principal message here is that despite what views on joy and happiness were expressed or the eloquence of the author, there hasn't been, and still isn't, any universal definition of joy and happiness that applies to all people at all times.

Plato (428/347 BC) said, *"The man who makes everything that leads to happiness depends upon himself, and not upon other men, has adopted the very best plan for living happily." Plato, The Republic*

Aristotle (384-322 BC) defined happiness as the ultimate purpose of life, where it depends on the attainment of moral character requiring intellectual contemplation through rational capacities.

Jeremy Bentham (1748-1832) proclaimed that, "the common end of every person's efforts is happiness"; or Herbert Spencer (1820—1903) who said, "Without pleasure there is no good in life"; or James Ward (1843–1925), who said that the sole aim of a sociology is the organization of happiness.

Carl Andreas Hilty (1833–1909) stated, "Whatever the philosophers may say, it remains true that, from the first hour of man's waking consciousness until that consciousness ceases, his most ardent desire is to be happy, and that the moment of his profoundest regret is when he becomes convinced that on this earth perfect happiness cannot be found."

Henry Thomas Hamblin (1873–1958) said, "This desire for happiness is good, for it leads us through innumerable experiences so that the soul can realize, by practical experience, the emptiness of all self-seeking, and thus, learn wisdom. After running the whole gamut of experience, the soul learns at last that happiness is not something that can be found by seeking it, but is an inward mental state."

It's obvious, from these samples, there remains no clear definition of what makes up happiness and how to achieve it.

IMPORTANCE OF JOY AND HAPPINESS

Joy and happiness have more importance than just an emotional state or feeling good; both are also important to your

- health,

- longevity,

- success,

- relationships.

- friends,

- family, and

- employer.

As Beata Souders, MSPP, ACC, said, "Psychological wellbeing is no longer understood as only the absence of mental illness, but also conceptualized as the simultaneous presence of positive psychological resources".

Health and wellbeing is enhanced, according to Shelley Taylor, through the cultivation of psychosocial resources of:

- optimism,

- social support,

- sense of mastery,

- self-esteem, and

- active coping skills.

In recent years, the fields of psychology and mental health have shifted focus from simply treating mental illness to emphasizing the importance of well-being and happiness. This shift has led to the development of a new branch of psychology: Applied Positive Psychology (APP).

Not only does APP address the best ways to help people with mental illness, but it also addresses how we can help everyone else learn how to be happier and healthier in their lives. Researchers are now studying how to improve our quality of life, increase well-being, and enhance resilience among individuals and whole communities.

On the road to pursue joy and happiness, I will discuss the following elements:

1. Developing Resilience
2. Embracing Spirituality
3. Eliminating Negative Self-talk
4. Overpowering Imposter Syndrome
5. Setting Healthy Boundaries
6. Success
7. Surmounting Circumstances
8. Hard Work
9. Knowing Yourself
10. Overcoming Worry
11. Why Mindfulness
12. The Truth About Money, Wealth
13. Benefits of Ethics, Morals
14. Banish Fear of Failure
15. Using Time Wisely
16. Not Blaming Others
17. Age Doesn't Matter
18. Incorporating Smiling, Laughter
19. Beneficial Friendships

Each element will conclude with an *appropriate habit*. Please note that there isn't just one habit that is more important or more vital than any other. Often, it is a combination of many habits that will give you the means to move forward in your quest for a joyful and happy life.

DEVELOPING RESILIENCE

Resilience is the ability of humans to cope with their environment and the ability to recover from tough experiences. Resilience is a quality of inner strength that allows us to persevere through difficult circumstances, such as a job loss or illness. Faced with negative challenges, resilience helps us stay positive and remain focused on our goals despite the obstacles.

Here's why resilience is important to you.

A resilient person will embrace a setback as an opportunity for growth instead of giving up. They understand they can turn negative events into positive ones and learn from mistakes. This mindset helps them to build stronger relationships with others along the way and gain new insights about themselves that they may not have found otherwise. With resilience comes greater confidence in oneself, which leads to more happiness and well-being overall.

Ways To Improve Resilience

Resilience is incredibly important for mental and physical health, especially when faced with stressors. Building resilience can be challenging, but there are several suggestions that may help one become more resilient.

1) Remember what processes that you used in the past that were successful in overcoming a particular challenge or resolve a troublesome issue. Actively thinking about how to replicate these processes can help build resilience in the face of future challenges. Why is this beneficial? Because it allows us to identify the skills and strategies that helped us before and apply them again in the future.

2) Develop a strong support system of friends, family, and colleagues that helps bring perspective and support during difficult times.

3) Self-care contributes to improving resilience as it provides a sense of control over one's own well-being and stress levels. This includes getting plenty of good sleep, eating nutritious meals regularly, exercising according to personal abilities, practicing mindfulness activities such as yoga or meditation, or just taking time out each day to relax with hobbies like reading or drawing.

As life becomes more unpredictable, resilience is becoming a necessary tool to help navigate the future. Research has found that resilience can be learned and cultivated, meaning that anyone can learn the skills needed to bounce back from challenging times.

A deep sense of optimism is essential for building resilience. Having strong social support mechanisms (friends, family) can help us build up our reserves during challenging times.

Habit # 1: Building resilience is a key habit to develop to meet life's issues and challenges head-on. By using past strategies to overcome new challenges, developing a strong support network of friends and family, and realising that you have the inner power to work through adverse conditions is an important road to travel.

EMBRACING SPIRITUALITY

———

In many world religions, joy and happiness are connected with spirituality. It has been well-documented that there are many benefits of using spirituality to promote joy and happiness and overall well-being.

Please note that the following are only a few examples of world religions and are, therefore, not meant to be an exhaustive presentation.

World Religions

The world is home to many religions and spiritual practices, each of which has its own unique set of beliefs and values. Although a wide variety of religious traditions exist, there are some major religions that are most popular worldwide. The five dominant world religions—Christianity, Judaism, Islam, Hinduism, and Buddhism—have the largest number of adherents in the world today.

Christianity

Christianity is one of the most widely practiced religions in the world. It is based on the teachings of Jesus Christ and has millions of followers around the globe. Christianity teaches its believers that faith, love, and hope are essential for living a life that's pleasing to God and brings joy to themselves and those around them.

For Christians, joy comes from having a strong relationship with God through Jesus Christ. To achieve this goal, many devote themselves to worshiping him through prayer and reading His word (the Bible). Also, regularly attending in fellowship with other believers in church offers them encouragement and helps them better understand how to live out their faith.

This understanding provides them with peace, contentment, joy, security, love, purpose, and meaning in life - all components necessary for true spiritual happiness. It does not mean these doctrines are a list of rules and regulations as legalistic religions might teach. These fundamental beliefs are a description of the character and nature of God that helps us understand His will for us.

Judaism

The religion of Judaism is a major part of joy, happiness and spirituality for many people. It has played an important role in shaping history, culture, and morality in the Middle East and around the world. Judaism focuses on God's laws in the Torah. Those who practice Judaism draw on its tenets to guide their daily lives.

Those practicing Judaism strive to find joy, peace, and contentment through following its teachings, such as treating others with respect and kindness, studying sacred texts, observing religious holidays, maintaining prayer rituals, visiting holy sites, and taking part in community events. This connection helps bring comfort, meaning, and purpose to life; becoming manifest in day-to-day spiritual practices that foster greater awareness of self and others.

Judaism originates from Israel approximately 3,000 years ago. This faith is based on the concept that God chose the Jewish people to be His chosen vessels after revealing Himself through Abraham. Jesus Christ is not seen as a divine figure in Judaism, but is viewed as a skilled teacher who lived an exemplary life amongst his peers.

Islam

Islam existed for centuries. For many believers, Islam is not simply a religion; it is also a way of life that brings joy, peace, and spiritual fulfillment.

There are five pillars of Islam that are the foundation of the faith. First pillar: called Shahadah, which means belief in one God and acceptance of Muhammad as his prophet. Second pillar: known as Salah, or prayer, which includes five daily prayers and a weekly congregational service on Friday. Third pillar: Zakat or charity. Muslims are expected to donate 2.5% of their income to the needy and to those in need. Fourth pillar: Sawm, also known as fasting during the month of Ramadan. The fourth pillar is considered the most important of all five pillars. It is a time when Muslims recognize their dependence on God and seek to cleanse themselves of their sins. And finally, the fifth pillar is Hajj, or pilgrimage to the holy city of Mecca.

Hinduism

Hinduism dates back thousands of years. The holy texts and scriptures of Hinduism offer many paths to spiritual enlightenment and lasting happiness. Hindus believe that creating harmony between physical, mental, emotional, and spiritual realms will bring joy and abundance into one's life. Through meditation, prayer, and contemplation, practitioners can access inner peace and an appreciation for life's blessings.

The central focus of Hinduism is living in alignment with dharma - a Sanskrit term meaning "duty" or "path" - which encourages individuals to act in accordance with their true nature. It holds that by fulfilling this innermost duty, we can achieve lasting contentment. It also teaches believers to look at their lives from a more holistic perspective so that they can find balance, even when times are difficult.

Habit # 2: The habit of practicing a certain spiritual belief is not a once in a while way of life. It is a daily adherence of belief that can bring people joy and satisfaction in life. It provides a sense of purpose, hope, and peace that is scarce in other areas of life.

ELIMINATING NEGATIVE SELF-TALK

———

Negative self-talk is a common phenomenon. It is a type of internal dialogue in which an individual speaks to themselves in an overly critical and harsh way. Negative self-talk can manifest itself as insults, putdowns, and belittling remarks that an individual makes about themselves. This can be done either consciously or subconsciously, but it serves to decrease the individual's self-confidence and esteem.

Negative self-talk can take a variety of forms, such as

- focusing on mistakes made rather than successes

- taking responsibility for situations beyond one's control, or

- setting unreachable goals that are focused on perfectionism.

They have linked this type of negative internal dialogue to depression, anxiety, low performance at school or work, and even physical symptoms like headaches and fatigue.

The Relation Between Negative Self-talk and Depression

Negative self-talk is a normal part of being human, but it can also have serious consequences. Research shows that there may be a link between negative self-talk and depression.

Studies suggest that people who experience higher levels of negative self-talk are more likely to develop symptoms of depression. The study also found that these thoughts usually focus on feelings of guilt or inadequacy, and happen in moments when the person is feeling low or stressed out. Negative self-talk can become an unhealthy coping mechanism in times of distress, leading to further problems.

Negative Self-talk and Doubt

Doubt can be self-talk too, but is often rooted in fear or anxiety.

The main difference between self-talk and doubt lies in the intention behind each statement. Positive self-talk is intended to empower us; it's about believing in our own abilities and potential for success. Conversely, doubt may come from a place of fear; it's negative and puts limitations on what we think we can achieve.

For example, doubt might sound like, "This will never work." Whereas, negative self-talk might sound like "I'm not able to accomplish that assignment" or "I'm unable to finish this project on time".

How To Stop Negative Thoughts

Negative thoughts can be hard to shake, but it's important to remember that you have the power to stop them. Everyone experiences negativity from time to time, and it can have a detrimental impact on our physical and mental health. Fortunately, there are solutions available that can help us put an end to the spiral of negative thoughts.

The first step is realizing *when* these negative thoughts enter your mind. Once you notice them, you can start working on finding solutions to eliminate them.

8 Recommendations To Curb Negative Self-Talk

First, develop attentiveness so that you *recognize* a negative thought, and take notice *when* you experience one.

Second, challenge your negative thoughts and re-state (reframe) them into positive ones. Instead of focusing on *what could go wrong*, think about *what could go right*. Or, for example, instead of saying "I will do my best to complete this project despite not knowing how to proceed" say "I'll get it done because I can figure it out".

Third, practice mindful meditation or relaxation techniques, such as deep breathing or progressive muscle relaxation. This will help clear your mind.

Fourth, talk to someone who understands what you're going through, like an understanding colleague, friend or family member who can provide comfort and reassurance that you have progressively developed in your career. Accept their compliments and be grateful for what you have achieved.

Fifth, get more involved in activities that make you feel good about yourself, such as sports or volunteering. This will foster positive experiences and give purpose to life.

Sixth, practice mindfulness and be more aware of your thoughts rather than allowing them to run rampant through your mind without question. The point is to question the validity or truthfulness of the thought. For example, if your thought is "I'm not good with this type of job", ask yourself if there is any evidence that proves your thought is wrong. For example, "Did my boss or colleagues recently praise me for a similar job that I completed?"

Seventh, take some time out if you're feeling overwhelmed by stress or anxiety. Perhaps spend an hour relaxing with a book or listening to calming music or taking a long walk through a park or nature.

Eight, create a '*stop sign*' thought. Whenever you have a negative thought, firmly tell yourself that it isn't productive and refocus on something positive instead.

—————

Benefits of Positive Thinking (as opposed to negative self-talk)

The Mayo Clinic (mayoclinic.org) staff suggest that the health benefits that positive thinking brings may include:

- Increased life span

- Lower rates of depression

- Lower levels of distress and pain

- Greater resistance to illnesses

- Better psychological and physical well-being

- Better cardiovascular health and reduced risk of death from cardiovascular disease and stroke

- Reduced risk of death from cancer

- Reduced risk of death from respiratory conditions

- Reduced risk of death from infections

- Better coping skills during hardships and times of stress

—————

Here are some examples of putting positive thinking into practice. As I mentioned earlier, don't expect that positive change will begin immediately. However, with consistent practice over time, eventually your self-talk will be less critical and become a valuable new habit.

—————

<u>**Negative Self-talk**</u> ——— <u>**Positive Self-Talk**</u>

I've never tried to do that before.	*Here's my chance to learn a valuable new skill.*
It's too difficult.	*I'll divide it into smaller steps that I can easily accomplish.*
I don't have the supplies that I need.	*I'll ask my friends if they have any suggestions.*
I'm already overwhelmed to get it done.	*I can readjust my priorities to get it done.*
This idea just won't work.	*There is no harm in giving it my best to make it work.*
That change is too outlandish for it to work.	*I'll ask for clarification on the steps I should take to accomplish it.*
Why doesn't anyone talk to me?	*I'll talk with people to see if I can find common ground to build further discussion.*
I don't think I can master the skills needed.	*I'll attempt to complete the project and get help when I need it.*

When your thinking is positive, you'll be better able to cope with minor stresses in a productive way. When you're feeling down, you'll be more likely to look for the positive in whatever situation you're dealing with. You'll be more likely to bounce back from stressful events instead of getting stuck in them.

But, let me repeat myself. Don't expect immediate or sustained positive change. Like the development of any new habit (and *positive thinking is a habit* and not a onetime behavior), consistent practice over time will lead to less self-criticism and a more positive outlook, with associated behaviors, on life and its changing challenges.

Habit # 3: Change your inner dialogue and establish a life-changing habit. Be mindful of what and when you engage in negative self-talk and change into positive affirmations.

OVERPOWERING IMPOSTER SYNDROME

Imposter Syndrome (IS) is a psychological phenomenon that can affect anyone, regardless of their accomplishments or successes. Imposter Syndrome was first identified in the late 1970s by two clinical psychologists, Dr. Pauline Clance and Dr. Suzanne Imes.

IS can lead to feelings of inadequacy and self-doubt because of the belief that any success achieved is simply luck or accidental. People who experience this condition may feel like they are not worthy of the recognition they receive, even though they have accomplished impressive results.

Those who suffer from IS may be highly successful in their fields but still struggle with insecurity, worrying that others will eventually uncover their true identity as an 'impostor' and deem them unworthy of praise or recognition. This can cause anxiety, stress, and depression, as these individuals constantly question themselves while striving for perfectionism.

This can happen to anyone regardless of occupation, race or gender. It can manifest itself in different forms, such as feelings of inadequacy, lack of self-confidence, and difficulty in accepting compliments or praise.

Individuals who suffer from imposter syndrome may struggle with achieving true contentment or happiness because of their inability to be proud of themselves and doubt their own skills. They have unrealistic expectations for themselves, leading them to stay trapped in this cycle that prevents them from feeling satisfied with the success they have achieved. They may also experience anxiety when attempting something new because they are certain that they will fail before even trying.

Causes of Imposter Syndrome

External pressures may cause IS, such as feeling the need to live up to others' expectations, or comparison with others, leading one to feel inadequate.

Internal pressure may also cause it, such as having high standards for oneself and setting goals that may be difficult to achieve.

Six Known Types of IS

The first type is called The *Superwoman/man Complex*, which is characterized by feeling pressure to overachieve and constantly prove one's worthiness. Individuals often feel inadequate even when they have accomplished great things, expecting others to recognize their achievements but believing they still don't measure up.

The second type is called *The Perfectionist Trap*, which can manifest itself in various ways, such as striving for perfection or having an unrealistic standard for one's own performance.

The third type is called *The Dependent Man/Woman Complex*, in which one feels the need to depend on another person or external support in order to function and feel okay.

The fourth type is called *The Insecure Man/Woman Complex*, which is an exaggerated fear of loss or rejection.

The fifth type is called *The Inappropriate Man/Woman Complex*, which is characterized by the feeling that one has to be in control at all times.

The sixth type is called *The Imposter Complex*, which refers to a fear of being found out as a fraud or phony.

Impact on Mental Health and Well-being

Happiness and IS have a complex relationship, with happiness often being diminished or suppressed by IS. As a result, it's important to understand how they interact in order to increase our mental health and well-being.

As we've learned, IS means feeling inadequate despite external recognition of competence. This can lead to:

- fear of failure,

- extreme self-criticism,

- intense pressure, and

- stress.

Specific Signs and Symptoms

It is important to note that these symptoms may vary based on an individual's unique circumstances; however, some common signs include

- feeling overwhelmed by assigned tasks,

- depression,

- shame,

- guilt,

- convincing oneself that failure is imminent, no matter the effort expended, and

- feel as though their success will never be acknowledged or celebrated.

Practical Coping Tips

IS can be overcome by developing healthy coping mechanisms, such as

- changing (reframing) negative thoughts into positive ones,

- building self-confidence through accomplishments and achievements,

- learning to practice mindfulness,

- developing a support system to manage feelings of inadequacy or worthlessness, and

- engaging in a physical activity that helps reduce the stress associated with these symptoms.

Habit # 4: Recognize signs of Imposter Syndrome. Use the aforementioned practical tips to reduce or eliminate its negative impact and recognize the joy and happiness that you already possess in your life.

SETTING HEALTHY BOUNDARIES

Finding a balance between a life of joy and happiness, along with suitable boundaries, is an ongoing challenge. It's essential to establish healthy and reasonable limits on what we give and accept, while also striving for contentment.

One way to achieve this balance is to focus on both our needs and those of others. Establishing personal boundaries is important in creating meaningful relationships with ourselves, as well as those around us.

It's crucial that these boundaries don't prevent us from seeking joy in life or connecting with others. Relationships with family, friends, colleagues, etc., can bring immense joy into our lives if kept healthy through mutual respect and understanding of each other's needs or expectations.

It could mean expressing the need to enjoy some private time - or self-time - separate from your spouse or significant other. It is important to remember that personal limits vary depending on one's individual needs and values.

It is important to highlight that when you expect certain boundaries to be accepted so you should also respect the boundaries set by someone else in your family or social circle.

Types Of Boundaries

There are five different boundaries that must be considered, whether when you are in your work environment, associating with friends or colleagues, when you live alone, or when you are at home with your family.

Knowing the different boundaries and how they apply to you can help you protect your emotional and physical safety.

1) *Physical:* These deal with your body, such as controlling who touches you, how close people can stand to you in a conversation, or a designated private space or time period within a home in which to relax.

2) *Mental:* These control what thoughts and ideas you will accept from others. This includes agreeing not to discuss certain topics or accepting someone else's opinion without question.

3) *Emotional:* These regulate how much emotion you allow yourself to display in public settings or with certain people.

4) *Spiritual:* These define what kinds of beliefs and values you're willing to accept for yourself or for those around you.

5) *Financial:* These specify thoughts and actions about money. For example, thoughts and behaviors around saving money, refusing to spend money just to be trendy, loaning to family or friends, or how much and when to give to certain types of charities.

———————————

Habit # 5: Establishing boundaries (limits) can help us distinguish between what we expect and what we expect from others so that we can maintain good relationships with others and create a healthy lifestyle.

SUCCESS

———

Success and happiness are two of the most sought-after goals in life. They are often intertwined, but not always mutually exclusive. To some, accomplishments such as wealth, fame or a fulfilling career measure success. For others, happiness comes from contentment with a simpler lifestyle. No matter how you define success and happiness, there are certain steps you can take to achieve them both.

Be conscious of setting realistic goals that align with your values and passions. This will help provide direction and focus on what truly matters in life rather than chasing material possessions or external validation.

It's equally important to practice self-care and make time for activities that bring joy into your life each day, no matter how busy your schedule may be.

Does success prevent one from experiencing true happiness, or is it possible for successful people to be content with their lives?

In order to answer this question, it is necessary to explore the various elements which make up a successful life.

Success can come in many forms - wealth, power, fame, recognition, and even personal satisfaction. However, these are all external achievements that do not lead to internal stability or contentment. Financial security may provide comfort and safety in life, however, it cannot guarantee inner peace or joy if one's relationships and personal life suffer due to neglect.

Defining Success

To achieve either, there must first be a definition of what defines success and happiness for an individual. For many, success is determined by achievements that have been reached throughout the course of their lives. Goals can help to set a path towards these accomplishments, while also providing motivation to keep pushing forward even when obstacles arise.

It's also important to look at both short-term and long-term objectives.

Short-term goals offer smaller victories, which often lead to larger accomplishments in the long run; for example, saving money for retirement or studying hard for exams in order to get into college or university.

Long-term goals may involve bigger changes, such as completing a degree or buying a house. These successes provide tangible results but require long-term dedication.

Connecting Success and Happiness

But what is the connection between success and happiness?

We can find connecting success and happiness in an individual's values. Values serve as a personal set of guiding principles that help determine how one lives their life. When individuals align their actions with the values that are important to them, they have a greater sense of peace, satisfaction, and joy.

Values provide clear priorities for decision-making, which can lead to more successful experiences throughout life. For example, if someone values honesty, then they will make decisions that reflect this value, such as being truthful in conversations or taking responsibility for mistakes made.

This not only leads to improved relationships, but also increases trustworthiness, which is key to career growth and success.

For example, reaching to the pinnacles of success while drastically eroding your value of treating everyone the way you want to be treated may be in stark opposition. Or sacrificing family time and its requirements for supportive and loving interaction when excessive time is devoted to a career.

When personal values are in clear conflict with your view of success, your happiness is compromised. It is time to re-evaluate whether one (success or values) must be re-examined to coincide with one's definition of success and happiness.

Habit # 6: Establish clear and concrete steps you will take to maintain the balance between your personal values and success.

SURMOUNTING CIRCUMSTANCES

———

Some people let random circumstances rule their thoughts for the rest of their day. For example, they go to make coffee/tea and find there is none left. They start the day by sarcastically thinking, "Oh great, this is going to be a good day". Then, for the rest of the day, they allow minor inconveniences, unplanned challenges, or other less than ideal events to reinforce their original negative thought.

Or how about the time when someone cut you off in traffic? It seemed like they didn't even notice you and just plunged forward with no regard for anyone else. Instantly, the entire day was ruined, and you got increasingly upset as you drove.

Even after the initial incident, you found yourself annoyed with everyone on the road; constantly checking your mirrors out of paranoia. The rest of your day kept getting worse, with nothing but annoying colleagues and an over-demanding boss.

If this has happened to you, you have made a choice - a choice to allow your mind to dwell on an annoying circumstance.

Was there an alternative reaction? There was.

Instead, you have the power to control how you behave; to choose a different view of the situation. But, what you did was to choose to giveaway power, the power to control the rest of your day to someone else's action (the circumstance). You gave that person who cut you off the power to take control of your emotions for the rest of the day.

Instead, take back control; accept that you weren't in an accident or worse, weren't severely injured, and focus your mind on someone or something thing that made you smile and keep that bright and happy vision as you continue your day. By adopting this thought and mind process, you have changed how you interpret or react to life's circumstances and events.

If you allow one negative and random event to control your mind continuously, then you are setting yourself up to allow only negative events to be your companion for the rest of the day.

Habit # 7: A circumstance doesn't have any power over you until you give it. Keep your power by refusing to let a circumstance rule your life.

HARD WORK

In today's world of hustle and bustle, the relationship between hard work and happiness is a topic of debate among both employers and employees. Studies show that while hard work can lead to greater success, it doesn't mean it will lead to lasting satisfaction and contentment. To better understand this relationship, many researchers have conducted studies on work and happiness in recent years.

These studies suggest that there is a correlation between the two, but not always a direct one. While people who are engaged in meaningful work may experience more joy than those who are unfulfilled by their duties, it also appears that too much stress or overworking can actually undermine any potential sense of pleasure or satisfaction with one's job.

The following studies speak specifically about work and its relationship to happiness.

The first study, conducted by professors from the University of Sheffield, Australia, and the University of Warwick in England, sought to determine whether work can bring happiness. They concluded it does. To conduct their research, the scientists drew upon data from a survey conducted in the United Kingdom between 2002 and 2003, which included over 10,000 people aged 16 to 64.

The second study conducted by the University of Sheffield sought to determine the relationship between happiness and the gender of the employee. The researchers discovered women are happier at work than men, but only when they have an equal or greater number of educational qualifications than their male counterparts.

The third study by the University of Sheffield examined the relationship between happiness and job role. The researchers discovered that certain roles, such as those in human resources or marketing, contribute to higher levels of happiness than others, such as those in accounting or finance.

The fourth study by the University of Sheffield examined the relationship between happiness and company size. The researchers discovered that larger companies have lower levels of employee happiness than smaller corporations.

The fifth study in the United States by the University of Michigan explored the connection between happiness and gender. The results showed women reported higher levels of job satisfaction than men did.

The final study by the University of Southern Sydney, conducted in Australia, found that both happiness and job satisfaction differed depending on the type of work. The study concluded that those working in sales and customer service were happier than those in other professions.

Do any of these studies provide conclusive findings about the relationship between happiness and work? It doesn't appear that there is one overarching conclusion, particular to any one person or group of persons. So, what does this tell us?

If you are happy at work, keep doing what you're doing. Not every job may lead to a feeling or emotional state of happiness. If not, change your job or career.

Nor would it be unreasonable to assume that your job would provide moments during a day or week that give you a sense of enjoyment, pride, or accomplishment. But would any of these moments be called happiness? That's for you to decide.

Maybe you've asked yourself questions like:

1. Why do other people get ahead at work?
2. Why do other people receive greater pay increases or larger bonuses?
3. Why are some people successful even when the odds are stacked against them?
4. Why are some people always upbeat and happy even when facing challenges?

If you want to learn the answers, check out our book "Wings for Work: Learn How To Develop and Use The Three Key Qualities That Successful People Have Mastered".

You'll discover:

- the three qualities that successful people have mastered,

- a 30 point checklist for success,

- how to survive in the new team environment,

- 20 key questions to ask yourself to help develop a 'positive attitude', and

- how to prepare yourself to benefit from continuous change.

Or, if you find your job role completely unsatisfying, or you experience constant stress in your job, maybe it is time to see what alternative employment is available.

If you agree it is time to find a new job, it is time to develop a goal-setting plan to provide the action steps to achieve it. Attempting to go forward in finding a new career without a specific plan does not differ from trying to sail a ship without a rudder.

For detailed and straight-forward goal setting plans, check out our website for

"Wings for Goals How to Use Three Easy Steps to Change Your Life Forever".

You'll discover:

- three easy steps that can change your life forever

- actions that help keep you moving forward when you feel discouraged;

- seven critical success elements you need

- reasons people are unsuccessful and how to avoid being one of them; and,

- the benefits you gain by setting goals.

The question is this: how much do you enjoy your work? This is an important question because, as noted above, you are spending many hours at work. In fact, during a regular work week, you'll spend more time at work than you do at home. This means that if you have a spouse or a significant other, you'll spend more time with other people than you do with them.

Habit # 8: If you don't enjoy your work, it is time either to change your work habits or it is time to find alternative employment.

KNOWING YOURSELF

———

Knowing yourself is a lifetime journey of self-discovery and growth. Self-reflection, understanding your emotions, and exploring your values are key to developing a deeper, more meaningful relationship with yourself; it is an invaluable life skill. Every single person has their own unique story, strengths, skills and experiences. By recognizing these traits and incorporating them into your personal narrative, you can develop greater self-awareness, appreciation, and acceptance of yourself.

Self-knowledge is helpful in all aspects of life, from career decisions to relationships with others. In short, it helps us cultivate healthier lives. Being able to identify our core values allows us to shape our behavior in alignment with those values. This can lead to more meaningful relationships with people, as well as success in professional pursuits. Having a better understanding of ourselves makes it easier for us to communicate our thoughts and feelings openly, without fear or hesitation.

Why Journaling Works

Evidence for the benefits of journaling is abundant. In a study of people who kept daily journals for eight weeks, researchers found participants reported greater self-awareness, an increased ability to identify and express their feelings, and better relationships with others (Kraus, 2006).

What's the secret to the humble diary? It turns out journaling works on two different levels, having to do with both our *feelings* and our *thoughts*.

As Mira M. Newman said in the Greater Good Magazine's article, Aug. 18, 2020, "it's a way of disclosing emotions rather than stuffing them down, which is harmful for our health. So many of us have secret pain or shame that we haven't shared with others, swarming around our brains in images and emotions. Through writing, our pain gets translated into black-and-white words that exist outside of ourselves."

Tips on Journaling

If you want to get to know yourself better, journaling is a great way to do just that. Writing your innermost thoughts and feelings can be a powerful self-exploration tool, allowing you to discover more about who you are and what makes you tick.

Here are some tips on how best to use journaling as part of your journey of self-discovery:

First, it's important that when you journal, don't worry too much about structure or style. Just start writing and let whatever comes out flow naturally. Don't be concerned if the words don't always make sense, because this is all part of the process.

Second, allow yourself time for free writing; don't set a time limit. Simply write whatever comes into your mind without worrying about grammar or sentence structure.

Third, try to write two or three times a week but if you can't don't pressure yourself to do so.

Fourth, at the end of the week, review your journal to see if there are any patterns or recurring themes you can make sense of. For example, if you keep writing about a certain person or event, then this might be a topic worth exploring further.

Journaling doesn't need to end after doing it for a short time. In fact, you can continue doing it for years, and continue to gain insight into your thoughts.

Benefits of Journaling

Journaling is an effective way to gain insight into yourself and your life. It can help you notice your inner thoughts and feelings that you might not otherwise be aware of, as well as uncover patterns in your behavior that can provide valuable insight into how you are growing and changing. Writing things down allows for reflection on what's happening in the present moment and provides a safe space to explore your beliefs, values, hopes, and dreams.

Cultivating a deeper awareness of self helps prevent us from floundering in challenging situations. As Joey Hulin said, "It is the difference between being completely consumed by stress, and having the ability to notice when we feel stressed and then course-correct to be more grounded and balanced."

In addition, when we can understand the roots of our thoughts, emotions, and behaviors, we can begin consciously to make wiser choices.

We can also establish the groundwork for making better decisions in the future. These decisions depend on the quality of our awareness and the level of our self-management. In this way, the cultivation of self-awareness becomes a major factor in reducing the number of mistakes we make.

Note that journaling in also part of mindfulness and it is an ongoing process. It is a habit that requires consistent practice and sustained effort to see real results.

Self-reflection and honest conversations with yourself can help you gain insight into who you are so that you can live life more authentically, with more vitality, and with a greater sense of joy and happiness.

Other Ways To Know Yourself Better

Here are some other tips for how to gain a better understanding of your thoughts and motivations.

1) Start by looking inward and focusing on your strengths and weaknesses.

2) Identify the areas that you feel passionate about.

3) Identify those areas where you could use improvement.

Ask yourself key questions such as:

- When do I feel most alive?

- What drives me?

- What is my purpose in life?

Habit # 9: Get to know yourself better by developing a habit of journaling and you can;

- develop a greater sense of self-awareness,

- gain clarity on your values and goals, and

- build healthier relationships with others.

OVERCOMING WORRY

———

"There is only one way to happiness, and that is to

cease worrying about things

which are beyond the power of will."

Epictetus

Worry is a natural emotion that we all experience. However, if it becomes excessive and rules our lives, it can lead to mental health issues. Fortunately, there are steps we can take to reduce worry. In this section, we will explore practical tips on how to reduce worry in your life and create a healthier mindset.

Here's what we know about worry:

- worry never contributes to joy or happiness;

- it is unproductive;

- it drains our energy;

- it always focuses on what if's rather than what is; and

- it negatively affects those close to us because it creates a helpless state of mind for those who wish to help.

Here is a personal example. I have a friend that no matter what happens, she never allows herself to be happy. She is always concerned about tomorrow and what might happen. She constantly lives within a never-ending worry cycle.

One example of her never-ending worry cycle occurred when she bought her first home. She had diligently saved her money for many years so that she could afford the down payment on a house. After she occupied her home, I visited her, expecting that she would be full of joy because of what she had done. Instead, her words only conveyed worry, not satisfaction.

Her worry focused on thoughts about what would happen if she lost her job and couldn't pay her mortgage. She focused her present thoughts on the problems that tomorrow might bring and not on the joy and accomplishment of the day. In this way, she was the catalyst for misery, with no grounding in reality. Her worry was about something she had no immediate control over, leading her to be filled with anxiety instead of joy.

From the example above, her focus was not on *what she could solve*. In order to solve her worry about the possibility of losing her job, *an action she could take* would be to ensure that her work qualifications are exactly what her employer needs. If not, she could enrol in additional courses that would ensure her value for her company or organization.

Practical Tips to Defeat Worry

So, let's move our discussion to exploring what practical tips help to defeat worry.

As in the above example, the first thing we should ask is whether the so-called worry is solvable?

We should define a solvable worry as an action(s) that can be taken immediately to address the specific worry. If you wish, you may invite a trusted friend, family member, or colleague to assist you in examining possible solutions.

Here is a *Four-Step* process to help you defeat worry:

- **Brainstorming**. This means thinking of *ALL* the solutions possible. Do not judge each solution on its worthiness, application, or whether it is the perfect one.

- **Evaluation**. Take each solution and determine if any solution or solutions would eliminate the worry if it was implemented.

- **Action Plan**. Take one of your solutions from the 'evaluation' stage and develop an action plan to put this solution into motion. This plan must be specific with details of what action or actions to take (these steps are the same as you would use if you were writing a goal-setting plan).

- **Take Action**. Your plan will only work if you take action. You need to start with one step at a time until you have taken all the action steps are required to reach your goal.

So, what about unsolvable worries?

If you are a worrier, the following words may not be comfortable to read, but it is time that you accept uncertainty as part of life. The main issue is this: casting worry upon situations or circumstances does not prevent undesirable surprises or troublesome occurrences from happening. Focusing on the '*what if this happens*' scenarios will only prevent you from enjoying the good things you already possess.

Refocus Your Mind Tips

Don't allow your thoughts to be mired in worry. Refocus your thoughts on other activities; activities that replace worrisome pictures in your mind with activities that give you a positive activity to dwell on, such as:

- engaging in household chores that need to be done and distract your mind. Simple things like vacuuming, dusting, laundry, potting new plants, outside gardening;

- take your mind and body outside for a walk in the park, around the neighbourhood, lift weights, yoga, or other physical activity;

- reading a book, magazine, newspaper, or travel to new locations around the world through the Internet;

- tackling reorganizing a room in your home, garage, or workshop;

- turning on a funny movie or listen to music that you enjoy; or

- engaging in a creative activity, such as oil or acrylic painting, writing, or a hobby that demands your focus or concentration.

And, it is vital to look after yourself (self-care) by incorporating practices that maintain mental and physical health, such as

- physical fitness such as walking, running, skating, treadmill, etc.,

- proper nutrition (eliminating binge eating, junk foods, excessive alcohol),

- channel worry into creative activities,

- active participation in spiritual practices and fellowship, and

- maintaining healthy relationships (you don't have to face life's challenges alone) with family members, friends, and co-workers.

You may already do some of the above activities. That's great. But do you mentally engage in any of them when worrisome thoughts consume you? The idea here is to make a conscious choice to turn your *worrisome thoughts* into *positive thoughts* by rechannelling your energy away from worry.

Habit # 10:

(a) If what you worry about is solvable, do so by taking specific and planned action. Refocus your mental energy for the best beneficial outcome. Develop the habit of transforming worry into positive thinking and action.

(b) If your worry is unsolvable, accept uncertainty as part of normal life and redirect your energy toward activities that engage the positive side of you for a joyful outcome.

WHY MINDFULNESS

———

For those who are new to mindfulness, it involves focusing on the present moment without judgement or expectations. To practice mindfulness, an individual should take time to be still and observe their thoughts and feelings without trying to change them or make them go away.

Mindfulness is a powerful tool for improving mental, emotional, and physical well-being. Developing mindfulness can help individuals to become more aware of the present moment and cultivate a deeper connection with their environment. Practicing mindfulness has multiple benefits that can positively impact our everyday lives.

Taking part in activities such as mindful eating, yoga, meditation, deep breathing exercises, or simply taking a walk can all be beneficial ways to develop greater awareness and presence in one's life.

Health Benefits of Mindfulness

Mindfulness has been gaining in popularity to manage stress and increase well-being. But did you know that mindfulness can also have significant health benefits?

Recent studies have shown that practicing mindfulness regularly can help reduce the risk of certain physical and mental illnesses, improve the body's ability to manage stress, and even increase longevity.

The Relationship Between Mindfulness and Longevity

A new study suggests that a mindful lifestyle can have a huge impact on longevity, leading to improved physical health and increased life expectancy.

Experts from Harvard Medical School conducted the research. They investigated the relationship between mindfulness practices and long-term health outcomes using data from over 75,000 participants. The results showed that those who practiced mindfulness techniques regularly had lower levels of stress hormones in their bodies, which resulted in better cardiovascular health and improved immune systems.

Additionally, individuals with higher levels of mindfulness were found to have greater resilience when it came to dealing with chronic illnesses such as diabetes or cancer.

Another study conducted by the University of the Wisconsin School of Medicine and Public Health found that practicing mindfulness techniques can help those with chronic pain experience less stress in their lives and make it easier for them to cope with the condition.

Additional studies said that when individuals practice mindfulness, it can help them control their actions, behaviors, and emotions more effectively.

Mindfulness is a useful tool for everyone to have in their arsenal. It's not just for those of us who are dealing with stress or chronic pain.

Practicing mindfulness regularly is linked:

- to lower levels of cortisol–a hormone associated with stress
- to improved concentration,
- to resilience,
- to better communication skills, and
- to self-control.

Further, mindful meditation, according to a review of literature cited in the National Library of Medicine, "Alterations in brain and immune function produced by mindfulness meditation: concluded that "These findings demonstrate that a short program in mindfulness meditation produces demonstrable effects on brain and immune function".

Tips for Practicing Mindfulness

Practicing mindfulness can provide many benefits, including increased focus, reduced stress levels, and improved relationships with others. Here are some tips for developing mindful practices:

1 - **Start small.** Take five or ten minutes each day to observe your surroundings without judgment or expectations. Focus on your breathing, being aware of each inhale and exhale.

2 - **Schedule time for yourself.** Make sure that you are carving out moments to slow down and practice mindfulness as part of your routine. You don't need to meditate for hours; even just a few minutes a day can make a difference in how you feel overall.

3 - **Be patient with yourself.** Don t be too hard on yourself. It is important to remember that mindfulness is a practice, not a product. There's no right or wrong way to do it, so don t stress if things don t go as planned.

4 - **Make it a habit.**

Workplace Benefits of Mindfulness

The power of mindfulness in the workplace can be a great asset to any business. By engaging in mindful practices, employees can become more productive and efficient at their jobs.

Benefits of mindfulness include:

- reducing stress levels,

- increasing overall well-being,

- improved focus, and concentration,

- better communication skills with coworkers and management,

- increased productivity due to improved efficiency in decision-making processes,

- increased creativity for problem-solving tasks,

- decreased likelihood of burnout from work-related stressors, and

- a greater sense of job satisfaction.

Mindfulness has been proven to help people achieve better physical health outcomes as well as improved mental health outcomes. A study conducted by the University of Massachusetts Medical School found that people who practiced mindfulness techniques had a lower risk of re-admittance to the hospital.

Practicing Mindfulness Exercises

1. **Yoga:** Yoga is the perfect way to practice mindfulness in your everyday life. By calming your mind and body, you can regain focus on the things that matter most to you. It's also a great way to relieve stress and get more out of life.

2. **Meditation:** Meditation is a great way to practice mindfulness, and we can do anywhere it. You simply focus on your breathing and slowly clear your mind of all the things that have been occupying your thoughts.

3. **Prayer:** Prayer is a great way to get in touch with your spirituality and connect with the things that matter most in life.

4. **Walking:** Walking is a great way to practice mindfulness. It's easy and relaxing and it allows you to have time for yourself with no distractions.

5. **Yoga nidra:** A yoga nidra session is a guided meditation that will help you feel more relaxed and focused.

6. **Qigong:** Qigong is a form of yoga that focuses on breathing and poses. It will help you relax and get more grounded in your day-to-day life.

Habit # 11: Mindfulness is a habit worthy of considering adding to your arsenal of mechanisms to help you appreciate being grateful for what you have and focus on personal growth with clarity.

THE TRUTH ABOUT MONEY, WEALTH

Money does not buy happiness."

Author Unknown

There have been many articles that indicate that wealth does not guarantee joy and happiness, so there is no need to dwell on this subject. Simply put, there are many unhappy people who have monetary wealth, and there are wealthy people who experience joy and happiness.

However, money cannot buy true friendship, nor health, nor cure any disease.

Many of us are wealthy in other ways. I know I am stretching the meaning of wealth, however, we all have other types of wealth that we simply do not recognize. Enjoy the wealth you already have in your family and friends, in your health, in your freedom, in your knowledge, and in yourself!

It is true that money can provide a certain level of convenience and comfort, but it cannot bring us lasting joy and emotional well-being. It is important to recognize that wealth is not the ultimate source of joy and happiness. We can attain meaningfulness in life, joy, and happiness regardless of income or material possessions.

Habit # 12: Focus on what truly matters in your life. Take a step back from materialistic desires and instead prioritize relationships, community, mental health, and other aspects of life that bring you lasting joy.

BENEFITS OF ETHICS, MORALS

Benefits of Doing The Right Thing

In this section, we explore the various ways in which doing the right thing can bring joy and satisfaction into our lives. Here, we will use the terms ethics and morals interchangeably. Simply note that ethics and morals can have different meanings depending on a specific or defined situation.

Ethics, according to the American Heritage Dictionary (AHD), is "the discipline dealing with what is good and bad and with moral duty and obligation." AHD also defines morals as "principles concerning the distinction between right and wrong or good and bad behavior.

In the application of ethics and morals, doing the right thing can have a multitude of benefits as it directly relates to the character of that particular person or group of people. It is important to remember that, when taking action, it is not only about what we gain from making a certain decision. It is about how our actions affect others.

Foremost, acting with integrity brings a sense of pride and accomplishment. By doing what is right and standing up for your beliefs, you can show both yourself and others your level of commitment to the values you hold; values that are important to you.

It is also significant that in order to maintain a consistent moral compass, your behaviors are consistent with an unchanging set of values. To change one's morals would be no different than saying that apples are your favourite fruit, but consistently eating oranges, or that stealing, which you hold to be wrong, is appropriate behavior only when you engage in it.

The benefit of maintaining a steady moral set of values, and the application of those values, is when we do something good for someone else or even ourselves. It can lead to feelings of gratification and an increased sense of self-worth.

The Link Between Morals & Happiness

The question is whether doing the right thing is essential for leading a life filled with joy and happiness?

Recent studies have shown that morality and joy and happiness have an undeniable link, with moral behavior often resulting in increased overall contentment. As humans, we want to do what is right; however, our desire for fulfillment and joy can sometimes influence us to act otherwise.

The importance of leading an ethical life has been long acknowledged by society at large; from religious texts to societal conventions. There are countless rules governing proper conduct in our behavior toward others. But having morals does more than just help one fit into their community, it also increases personal satisfaction and feelings of joy.

Research has proven that people who live according to moral standards are happier than those who don't. Research such as that done by Sonja Lyubomirsky and Todd Kashdan, two researchers at the University of California Riverside, supports this claim.

Another study by the University of Virginia (2014) found that people who exhibit moral behavior have higher levels of satisfaction and well-being. The concept of moral behavior is based on the idea that individuals can be held accountable for their actions. The researchers found that people who live according to their moral principles are happier than those who don't, and that when people act according to their morals, they feel happier and more satisfied.

As an example of written moral conduct, the Ten Commandments, as outlined in the Bible, were the foundation of Western civilization's moral code and have been a guiding force for many individuals.

In our quest for joy and happiness, we confront difficult ethical dilemmas that require us to make choices between right and wrong.

Challenges of Doing The Right Thing

Doing the right thing is not always easy. It can be a challenge to make hard decisions, especially when it involves our own personal joy and happiness. However, there are many rewards that come from doing the right thing despite the difficulties involved.

When faced with difficult choices, it's important to take time to think about what action would be best for ourselves and others in the long-term. Although our emotions can often lead us astray, we must remain focused on making decisions that will help bring lasting joy and contentment instead of short-term pleasure. Doing the right thing is an essential life skill if we want to find happiness and lasting joy in our lives.

Doing the right thing:

- builds character,

- increases self-confidence,

- strengthens relationships,

- helps to create a positive impact on society,

- brings a sense of pride and accomplishment,

- demonstrates your commitment to the values you hold

Habit # 13: Consistently doing the right thing is a habit worth establishing. It is not always easy, but it's always worth it. If you make a mistake, don't be too hard on yourself; learn from it and move forward. You can take small steps towards doing the right thing and gradually change your life to benefit you and those around you.

BANISH FEAR OF FAILURE

———

"The only thing to be feared is fear"

Lord Bacon

Fear of failure is a common yet complex emotion. It can have far-reaching consequences for an individual, impacting their performance in work, school and social situations. This fear can dramatically affect one's ability to find joy and happiness, especially if it is pervasive in many aspects of daily life.

Underlying Causes of Fear of Failure

To better understand this fear, we must first look at the underlying causes of the fear of failure. It is important to do this because, many times, the fear of failure is actually a combination of other insecurities.

The most common cause is low self-esteem; when someone lacks confidence in their abilities and skills, they become less likely to try something new. This lack of self-confidence can also lead to feelings of shame, which further contributes to a person's apprehension about attempting something that might fail.

Anxiety and Low Self-Esteem

Anxiety and low self-esteem can have a huge impact on our lives, influencing how we think and feel about ourselves. Often, people with these conditions suffer from the fear of failure, which can prevent them from achieving their goals or living life to its fullest potential.

It is important to understand that anxiety and low self-esteem are often two sides of the same coin; when one is present, so too is the other. Those suffering from anxiety may find themselves second-guessing every decision they make due to fear of failure or making mistakes.

When we have low self-esteem, we are always afraid that others will see our faults and ridicule us. Low self-esteem follows as a result of these worries and negative thoughts, leaving individuals without confidence in their own abilities.

The truth is, everyone experiences moments of anxiety and doubt in their lives. It is natural to feel overwhelmed by life's challenges and experience varying degrees of fear when facing unfamiliar tasks or goals. But rather than letting these fears hold you back from achieving your goals, it's important to develop healthy coping strategies that can help you overcome them.

Identifying Negative Thinking Patterns

Fear of failure can prevent people from taking risks, creating relationships, and pursuing goals that could lead to greater satisfaction and joy. To counteract this debilitating mental habit, it's important to identify negative thinking patterns that may be holding you back.

The first step in overcoming these thought processes is to be aware of them. Pay attention to your thoughts you feel anxious.

Ask yourself if your thoughts are helpful or harmful? Are they irrational and unhelpful? Recognize them as false beliefs or distorted reality and choose not to believe them.

Coping Strategies

Happiness and success in life come from taking risks, and facing your fears can ultimately be rewarding. Here are some coping strategies that can help you overcome the fear of failure:

- **First**, recognize that all failures contain an opportunity for growth. Acknowledge what didn't work out as planned, but focus on what you can learn from it. See mistakes as learning experiences instead of sources of shame or regret. Reframe negative situations into something positive by viewing them as chances for personal growth instead of as setbacks.

- **Second**, strive for progress over perfectionism.

- **Third**, don't focus on meeting impossible goals.

- **Fourth**, set realistic goals and be patient with yourself. Focus on achieving your step-by-step actions (one at a time) instead of the outcome.

- **Fifth**, remember that the hard part of a task is not having the talent for it; it's deciding to do it.

Positive Benefits of Taking Risks

Taking risks means facing the possibility of failure, but it also comes with many positive benefits that far outweigh any potential losses. By learning how to use risk-taking as part of an overall strategy, people can reap rewards, such as:

- increased self-confidence,

- improved problem-solving skills, and

- greater opportunities for personal growth.

Those who overcome this fear will often discover newfound courage and resilience while they take their first steps into the unknown. By embracing their fear and making conscious decisions to take calculated risks, individuals learn more about themselves and grow in ways not possible when playing it safe all the time.

We often focus on the end goal and forget to enjoy the journey along the way. There is satisfaction in successfully completing a specific action. As each step is completed, give yourself a mental pat on the back. Enjoy the journey one step at a time.

And, once you have accomplished your goal, you can set another one with even greater assurance that you are capable of achieving more. You do not live in the past; you live in the present on your way to future accomplishments.

With the right support (positive partners, family, friends), strategies, and resources, anyone can learn how to manage their fear of failure and find confidence in their own capabilities.

Failure is not the end, but only the beginning. Within every failure, there are golden nuggets of information or processes that can be utilized to help you re-load and begin again with more confidence.

Habit # 14: Adopt the habit of reducing or eliminating the fear of failure by setting realistic goals, being flexible, and allowing yourself to fail. It's important not to settle for less than you are capable of achieving.

USING TIME WISELY

Our frantic pursuit of increased speed and productivity pushes us into the productivity trap. We try to go beyond our limits to do more in less time, and then we use that extra time to do even more things that must be done, and then we repeat the cycle. We lose our capacity to think, feel, and be present in the moment. We talk about the importance of a work-life balance but don't do it.

What Does Work-Life Balance Mean?

Work-life balance is a term used to describe the relationship between the amount of time and energy we spend working and the amount of time and energy that is dedicated to our personal lives. It has become increasingly important in today's world, where people are often juggling multiple roles and responsibilities both at home and in their professional career.

Achieving a healthy balance between work and life:

- can lead to increased job satisfaction,

- improved mental health (less stress and anxiety),

- better interpersonal relationships,

- greater productivity, and

- overall better quality of life.

Time Management and Balance of Life

Maintaining a healthy balance between work, leisure time and family life can be challenging in our fast-paced society. It is important to develop effective time management skills that will help you maintain a satisfying level of productivity while achieving balance.

Time management is essential for managing stress levels and ensuring that your personal needs are met. Setting deadlines, developing strategies to prioritize tasks and delegating responsibilities can help you stay organized and on track with your goals.

Joy and happiness are essential parts of life, but often we don't have enough time to focus on them. We must learn how to manage our time in order to make space for the things that we enjoy.

Time management techniques such as setting deadlines, breaking tasks down into smaller chunks, and creating a schedule can help you stay on top of your work and ensure that everything gets done on time. But, is time management the real issue?

Is there a downside to using every moment of your time to squeeze in more and more work or activities, or things that you feel compelled to do but really don't want to?

Is there a solution to our misuse of time? Yes. Instead of doing more, _change what you do_ with the time.

Let's explore this strategy further.

Many of you will remember the old time management rules where you established a priority list.

> 1) Must get finished items were, 'A'. For example, that project or job that your boss needed finished ASAP;
>
> 2) 'B' items were those of less importance but still had to be done, but if they went unfinished until a day or two later, it would not result in severe consequences; and
>
> 3) 'C' items were things you would like to do, but if you didn't do them, there were absolutely no adverse consequences.

Here's the change that you can make (you _should_ make). These next steps are important:

● Eliminate as many items as you can from your 'B' list; that is the things that can wait.

● The time you save by eliminating 'B' list items should _not be reassigned_ for your 'A' list. If you reassign time saved to your 'A' list, you are simply chasing the productivity cycle, and you are no better off than before. Unfortunately, every time you use _free_ time and assign it to your 'A' list, you engage in the same behavior you were attempting to avoid.

Any time that you saved by re-working your 'B' list, use for your personal benefit, like:

● spending time in nature

● enjoying time with your family

● engaging in a fun social activity

● playing a round of golf, or other favorite sports

● reading that book you wanted to read, or,

● immersing yourself in your favourite hobby.

You may also consider identifying daily activities that are helpful for maintaining mental health, such as exercising or meditating.

Achieving a healthy balance between work and life can lead to increased job satisfaction, improved mental health, better interpersonal relationships, greater productivity, and overall better quality of life.

Habit # 15: Develop the habit of resisting the productivity trap. Instead, establish the practice of using freed up time for personal pursuits and not work.

NOT BLAMING OTHERS

Joy and happiness are your responsibility. Some people have a tendency to blame other people for the way they are feeling. Other people are not responsible for your feelings. You are. You own them. You control them.

Some people get caught in the trap of trying to satisfy everyone and end up, in return, becoming very unhappy themselves.

Trying to make other people happy is like doing your child's homework for them and expecting them to pass future tests. You can help them, share your knowledge and experience, but they are the ones who have to study. You cannot do it for them. The same principles apply to happiness.

Are Others To Blame For Our Lack Of Happiness?

It's easy to blame others for our unhappiness, especially if we feel like they're the cause. If your thoughts are, "Why did this happen to me?", you are engaging in what I call the "poor me syndrome". But is this really the case?

Is it possible that our own actions and attitudes are responsible for our lack of happiness?

Research has shown that how we perceive and interact with the world around us can affect our overall well-being and satisfaction in life. If we focus on negative aspects or people and events, this can lead to feelings of resentment or even depression.

In an extreme form, known as 'narcissistic' behavior, the Mayo Clinic says, "Narcissistic personality disorder is a mental health condition in which people have an unreasonably high sense of their own importance. They need and seek too much attention and want people to admire them. People with this disorder may lack the ability to understand or care about the feelings of others."

Symptoms of narcissistic personality disorder and how severe they are can vary (mayoclinic.org). People with the disorder can:

- Have an unreasonably high sense of self-importance and require constant, excessive admiration.

- Feel that they deserve privileges and special treatment.

- Expect to be recognized as superior even without achievements.

- Make achievements and talents seem bigger than they are.

- Be preoccupied with fantasies about success, power, brilliance, beauty or the perfect mate.

- Believe they are superior to others and can only spend time with or be understood by equally special people.

- Be critical of and look down on people they feel are not important.

- Expect special favors and expect other people to do what they want without questioning them.

- Take advantage of others to get what they want.

- Have an inability or unwillingness to recognize the needs and feelings of others.

- Be envious of others and believe others envy them.

- Behave arrogantly, brag a lot, and appear conceited.

It is easy to see how a 'narcissistic' person could easily blame others for their unhappiness.

Studies about blaming others have revealed some interesting information about the connection between happiness and how we view responsibility. In general, it's been found that people who blame external factors for their own mistakes or misfortunes tend to be less happy than those who are willing to take ownership of their actions.

The research suggests that life satisfaction often depends on our attitude toward accepting responsibility for ourselves and our lives. Those who are able to recognize when they make a mistake or experience a setback tend to deal with the adversity more effectively and find ways to move forward.

Conversely, people who consistently blame others (like a narcissist) for their problems may find themselves unable to cope as easily with life's challenges, leading them down a road of resentment and pessimism.

Taking responsibility also involves looking inward; examining yourself for faults or parts that need improvement rather than always pointing out flaws in others. Finally, accepting responsibility means being able to forgive yourself when you stumble along the way and understanding that everyone makes mistakes now and then.

Dr. Margee Kerr and others, as cited in the Journal of Personality and Social Psychology, concluded that "the people who blame others are less happy than other people, and they're less satisfied with their lives."

Habit # 16: Accept responsibility for your failures or shortcomings. This is an essential part of individual growth and happiness.

"When we cannot find contentment in ourselves

it is useless to seek it elsewhere."

Francois La Rochefoucald

AGE DOESN'T MATTER

Age and happiness. Do the two go together?

Almost 80 years later, a Harvard study started in 1938 found a strong correlation between men's flourishing lives and their relationships with family, friends, and community.

Other studies found that people's level of satisfaction with their relationships at age 50 was a better predictor of physical health than their cholesterol levels were.

"When we gathered together everything we knew about them about at age 50, it wasn't their middle-age cholesterol levels that predicted how they were going to grow old," said Robert Waldinger, director of the study, a psychiatrist at Massachusetts General Hospital and a professor of psychiatry at Harvard Medical School. "It was how satisfied they were in their relationships. The people who were the most satisfied in their relationships at age 50 were the healthiest at age 80. (news.harvard.edu)

Researchers at the University of California, San Diego and the University of Chicago studied data from more than 70 countries, over a five-year period, analyzed data gathered from interviews with over 5,000 adults of different ages.

They looked at factors such as marital status, health status, and income to explore whether age was related to happiness. Susan Charles found that, in general, older people tend to be happier than younger people. She also found this to be true across a number of different factors that are known to affect happiness levels. For example, both health and relationship status were found to have an effect on happiness.

"A landmark longitudinal study across the adult life span, the first of its kind, by Charles and USC Dornsife Professor of Psychology Margaret Gatz showed that negative emotions such as anger, anxiety, stress, and frustration, far from increasing as we get older, actually decrease steadily with age.

Positive emotions, such as excitement, pride, calm, and elation, remain stable across the lifespan. Only the very oldest group registered a very slight decline in positive emotions.": This means that as we get older, we have fewer and fewer negative emotions. However, the amount of positive emotions remains the same across age. (dornsife.usc.edu)

Further, as we age, our brains become increasingly wired to concentrate on the positive. A study at USC Dornsife, USC Leonard Davis School of Gerontology, and Stanford University shows that older people pay more attention to positive stimuli, such as images of babies or athletes celebrating, whereas younger people pay more attention to the negative.

Achieving Lasting Fulfillment

Achieving lasting fulfillment is an important goal in life, but it's challenging to attain. New research suggests that age may play a role in how we experience happiness. A study from the University of Oxford has explored the relationship between age and well-being, concluding that different generations have unique perceptions of what brings them happiness.

The findings suggest that happiness peaks for Baby Boomers aged between 50 and 70 years old, who define fulfillment through relationships with family and friends, travel experiences, and financial security.

By contrast, younger generations prioritize career success over other factors when defining their sense of well-being. The research found that Millennials are likely to sacrifice personal relationships in pursuit of work achievements, such as promotions or higher salaries.

Understanding how age affects our perception of fulfillment can help us identify what measures we need to take in order to achieve true satisfaction with life.

There are many ways to increase happiness at any age. Overall, if we take the time to make meaningful connections with others, show compassion and gratitude, set goals, practice self-care and stay active in our community, we can experience more lasting joy and contentment throughout our lives.

Habit # 17: Adopt the habit of embracing the moments where joy and happiness are found. Remember, happiness can be achieved at any age, but it is up to you to make the choice.

"Let us never know what old age is.

Let us know the happiness time brings,

not count the years."

Ausonius

INCORPORATING SMILING, LAUGHTER

Smiling

Smiling is a powerful tool that radiates joy and positivity. A genuine smile, one that reaches the eyes, has been found to affect us physically and emotionally. Studies have shown that smiling can positively influence our mood and even reduce stress levels.

The science behind smiles is quite fascinating. It's considered an automatic facial response by many researchers as they've discovered evidence of babies smiling in utero. Smiles can be contagious. When you see someone else smile, it triggers a reaction in your brain, making you more likely to return the gesture. This form of emotional connectedness has been studied extensively throughout history, leading some experts to believe smiling is instinctive rather than learned behavior.

Let's look at some reasons that smiling is better than frowning:

- It takes fewer muscles to smile than to frown.

- Smiling will relieve stress, whereas frowning increases stress.

- People are attracted to those who smile.

- Smiling is the first measure of non-aggressive behavior extended to another.

- Smile and your eyes lighten up. Frown and your eyes darken.

- It costs you nothing to smile but provides huge dividends in return.

Research has shown that smiles can be heard. A recent study conducted by the University of California, San Francisco, found that when participants listened to recordings of people speaking, they could accurately distinguish between recordings of people smiling and not smiling, even through the recordings.

Many telemarketing companies require that their telemarketers speak to their mirrored reflection so they can see their own facial expressions. If they are not smiling, they can see themselves in the mirror as a reminder to smile as they speak.

Next time you are talking on the phone, listen, and see if you can tell when the person is smiling.

Share your smiles. When you say good morning, smile as you say it—you'll notice the difference in how people react to you.

Laughter

Laughter is often referred to as the best medicine. Research has shown that laughing can have a number of positive benefits in both physical and mental health.

Physically, it can boost the immune system, reduce stress hormones, and increase endorphins, which act as natural painkillers.

Mentally, laughter can help improve mood and reduce anxiety by releasing endorphins which create a feeling of happiness.

And it can increase creativity and problem-solving skills by helping us to look at situations from different angles.

In terms of social benefits, laughter can be an important tool for connecting with others. It can break down barriers between people by creating a sense of unity in shared experiences. As well, it helps build relationships by creating trust and closeness between individuals.

The following benefits of laughter came from the Mayo Clinic. I have adapted their viewpoints below:

Short-term benefits:

Laughter can:

- enhance your intake of oxygen-rich air, stimulate your heart, lungs and muscles, and increase the endorphins that are released by your brain.

- activate and relieve your stress response.

- reduces stress.

Long-term effects:

Laughter may:

- improve your immune system. Laughter may relieve pain by causing the body to produce its own natural painkillers,

- make it easier to cope with difficult situations,

- help you connect with other people,

- improve your mood, and

- improve your self-esteem.

Habit # 18

(a) Develop smiling as your daily habit and reap multiple benefits.

(b) Develop laughter as a habit to improve your mood, stimulate your heart, boost your immune system, reduce stress hormones, and increase endorphins, which act as natural painkillers.

BENEFICIAL FREINDSHIPS

No person is a pillar of strength and wisdom unto themselves. We all need support at one time throughout our lives, even if only for a few minutes or occasionally. But, make no mistake, going it alone through life without a compassionate and helpful friend is like sailing into a storm without a sea-worthy boat.

To me, part of joy and happiness is knowing that I have a loyal friend or friends that can help me through difficulties or challenges. It is a person(s) who keeps you on track, who does not bring you down with negative thinking, or who does not cloud your potential with their own petty self-serving excuses.

Now, let me get right to the point. A friend who brings you down by always pointing out the negative, requires you to build them up without reciprocating, who sees the negative side of almost every situation, or who does not support you in any way, at any time, is really not the type of person you need. This type of person is more a liability than an asset.

The type of person you need as a friend is one who sees life as a gift and lives for each moment without being mired in negative thinking or the "poor me" syndrome.

This is a person who supports you to overcome obstacles in every aspect of your life; a person who you can count on to help you shift your focus away from feeling sorry for yourself and directing you toward ways or thoughts that move you closer to what you view as happiness. This is also a person who knows when to act, when to speak, or when to listen.

Think about what type of friends you associate with right now. Do they give you what you need? Do they help support you? Do they encourage you? Choose friends who are supportive and upbeat and who will help you stay focused on solutions when times get tough.

And don't forget that friendships go both ways. What you get, you should also be willing and able to give.

Habit # 19: Choose your friends carefully and disassociate with ones who drag you down.

21- DAY CHALLENGE

═══

I would encourage you to try this 21 day challenge.

For the next 21 days:

1. Keep a daily journal.
2. Record three things (big or small) that made gave you joy or made you feel happy.
3. Next to each entry, record why each thing/event/circumstance made you joyful or happy.
4. Focus only on the positive and not the negative occurrences.

Why is this beneficial? It causes you to focus on sources of gladness, goodness, and joy in your life, which steadily points to a mindset of positivity and gratitude.

Here are a few examples of what may bring you joy or happiness. I'm sure you can think of more.

● a child's hug,

● lunch with a friend,

● a good book you are reading,

● a laugh shared with someone,

● a smile you received or gave,

● a completed project ahead of target,

● a compliment from a boss or a co-worker,

● a promotion

● an action step you completed in your goal-setting plan, or,

● the natural beauty you saw.

At the end of the 21 days, go back and read your journal. This will help your mind focus on the good in your life rather than dwelling on the negative. It will surprise you with the joy and happiness in your life. And don't stop journaling after 21 days. Keep going and make it a *habit* to note the joy and happiness you already possess.

It truly is all the little things in life that bring true joy or happiness. When you add all the small joys and kindnesses together, joy and kindnesses that are with you more days than they are absent, your total will equal or exceed one piece of great fortune.

CONCLUSION

So, what have we learned about the road to joy and happiness?

Simply put, we are responsible for our joy and happiness. No one else. Yes, it can be daunting, but also incredibly liberating. If we take ownership of our joy and happiness, we are no longer dependent on outside forces to make us feel fulfilled.

We have the power to choose how we view life's events, big or small.

We have the option, the choice, to enjoy and appreciate what every day brings.

The good news is this: joy and happiness is a state of mind that can be cultivated through daily practices. It is possible to create a life full of joy and happiness by making small changes in your daily routine.

These small changes, and *the development of associated habits*, include practices that can range from simple activities, such as taking a walk in nature, to more complex ones like meditation, eliminating negative self-talk, and mindfulness.

They can also include spending time with family and friends, engaging in meaningful conversations, contributing to other people in need, or taking committed time away from the hustle and bustle of life and spending time on a favourite hobby like reading, listening to music, or doing anything that brings you happiness.

By incorporating these *habits* into our everyday lives, we can experience an overall sense of well-being and satisfaction with life; a sense of joy and happiness.

If we see life's challenges as stepping stones, as learning experiences, our opportunity for joy and happiness increase.

Unfortunately, for many people, they choose to postpone joy or happiness for a later date. They decide that they'll be happy after they finish school, buy a house, save a certain amount of money, or find the person of their dreams. This is a mistake. Being unhappy harms you and everyone else in your life.

Sometimes we forget to enjoy the present moment because we're too preoccupied with possible future outcomes.

And we all know someone who never seems to be happy; they always have something to complain about. When you and hear nothing but negative responses from them, ask them, "What one thing that happened today makes you joyful or happy?"

Don't let them off the hook. Insist that they tell you one thing. Remind them it is the little things in life that bring joy or happiness. This behavior helps them turn their attention away from negative thoughts to positive ones.

Summary of reasons that joy and happiness are important.

1. **Happy people are healthier.** Happier people get sick less frequently and less severe on the average than unhappy people. Happy people visit the hospital less frequently. Happy people are less likely to suffer from anxiety or depression. Your physical and mental health are at greater risk when you're unhappy.
2. **Happy people live longer.** Several studies suggest that the happiest people live up to 10 years longer than those that are the least happy. Also, since happy people are healthier, they also tend to live longer, too. Happiness can do more to boost your lifespan than just about anything else.
3. **Happy people are more resistant to stress.** Unhappy people are more easily overwhelmed when stressed. Happy people are better able to handle stress, and the effect that stress has on them decreases.
4. **Happy people enjoy stronger relationships.** Would you rather be around someone that was happy most of the time or someone that was not? Being happy can boost all of your relationships, including those with your partner, family, friends, and coworkers.

5. **Happy people get more done.** Happy people are more productive and are better employees.
6. **Happy people have more friends.** Happy people attract others. We enjoy being around people that are in a positive emotional state. We avoid those that aren't.

Understand this: the journey to lasting joy and experiencing happiness is ongoing, but the key starts with one person: YOU. Joy and happiness are determined by how you think about your life, how you act and react to the variety of issues, challenges, and circumstances of each day.

Final Words

Joy and happiness are **NOT** something *to be achieved*, but something to be cultivated. It is within our reach *if we make the effort to nurture it every day*. The road to joy and happiness is a journey, and it is this journey where all of life's blessings are experienced. To be sure, it means a journey where ruts and bumps are confronted, but it is also a journey filled with beauty and tranquillity.

True joy, happiness, and satisfaction comes from within, through connecting with our passions, developing meaningful relationships, practicing gratitude, contributing to the social well-being of others, living with a purpose, and sharing our joy.

"This is the beginning of a new day.

I have been given this day to use as I will.

I can waste it or use it. I can make it a

day long to be remembered for its joy, its beauty, and

its' achievement, or it can be filled with pettiness.

What I do today is important because

I am exchanging a day of my life for it.

When tomorrow comes, this day will be gone forever,

but I shall hold something which I have traded for it.

It may be no more than a memory, but if it

is a worthy one, I shall not regret the price.

I want it to be gain, not loss, good not evil,

success, not failure."

Author Unknown

JOY AND HAPPINESS QUOTES

I have included several quotes that talk about elements of joy and happiness. I have found from my experience that a certain quote or quotes remind me of what I already possess but have forgotten. They help me to refocus away from a current issue to a broader sense of well-being. There is more to life than a present circumstance, problem or headache. Life is full of a vast number of blessings, but only when we step back and out of our current dilemmas.

It's like having a collection of maps for different places. No matter which map you look at, it will show you the same destination, but each map offers a unique route to get there.

(Happiness is) "the experience of joy, contentment,

or positive well-being, combined with a sense

that one's life is good, meaningful, and worthwhile."

<u>*Sonja Lyubomirsky*</u>

"Outer changes always begin with

an inner change of attitude."

<u>*Albert Einstein*</u>

"Many persons have a wrong idea of what constitutes

true happiness. It is not attained through self gratification

but through fidelity to a worthy purpose."

<u>*Helen Keller*</u>

"Happiness is an attitude.

We either make ourselves miserable,

or happy and strong.

The amount of work is the same."

<u>*Francesca Reigler*</u>

"People are just about as happy as

they make their minds to be."

<u>Abraham Lincoln</u>

"Man is not asked whether he will accept life.

That is not the choice. You must take it.

The only choice is how."

Henry Ward Beecher

"Be happy while you are living, for

you're a long time dead."

Scottish Proverb

"If you enjoy what you do,

you will never work another day in your life."

Confucius

"There is work that is work and there is play that is play;

there is play that is work and work that is play.

And in only one of these lies happiness."

Gelett Burgess

"The most thoroughly wasted of all days is that

on which one has not laughed."

Nicolas Chamfort

"Happiness always looks small while you hold

it in your hands, but let it go, and you learn at once how

big and precious it is."

Maxim Gorky

"Happiness consists more in small conveniences

of pleasures that occur every day, than in

great pieces of good fortune that happen

but seldom to a man on the course of his life."

<u>*Benjamin Franklin*</u>

———————————

Each day is a gift; a day that is never repeated. It is yours to do with as you wish. I hope that your road to joy and happiness roots and grows to magnificent proportions.

———————————

Byron Pulsifer

A PERSONAL REQUEST

———

We'd love to hear what you thought of this book. For example, did it encourage you to change your thinking to handle issues or challenges, adopt a new behavior, or establish a new habit?

Or did we leave something out that was of concern to you? Or did we fail to explain something?

Your comments and opinions are important to us. They help us write about issues and concerns in future books that are important to you.

Thank you. We appreciate your help.

Please send your opinions and comments to:

byron@pulsiferbooks.com

———

Byron and Catherine Pulsifer

———

For more inspiring quotations and short poems, please visit our website:

https://stresslesscountry.com Short Poems and Quotes

OTHER PULSIFER BOOKS

https://pulsiferbooks.com

WINGS *for* GOALS:

How to Use Three Easy Steps to Change Your Life Forever!

by Catherine Pulsifer

https://books2read.com/u/boylYa

Have what you've always wanted! Some people seem to have all the luck. They always seem to get what they want—wealth, possessions, career. How do they do it?

Learn how to get what you want, desire, or need in your life.

You will discover:

- 3 easy steps that can change your life forever

- 3 actions that help keep you moving forward when you get discouraged

- 7 critical success elements you need so you can get what you want

- 7 reasons why people are unsuccessful and how to avoid being one of them

- 14 benefits you gain by setting goals

WINGS *for* WORK:

Learn How to Develop and Use the Three Key Qualities that Successful People Have Mastered! by Catherine Pulsifer

https://books2read.com/u/bMNNQG

Have you ever wondered why other people get ahead at work, or why they receive greater pay increases or larger bonuses? Stop wondering and join them.

Here's what you'll learn:

- the three qualities that successful people have mastered
- a 30 point checklist for success
- what you need to know to survive in the new team environment
- 20 key questions to ask yourself to develop a positive attitude
- how to better prepare yourself to benefit from continuous change

---

WINGS of WISDOM:

Your Daily Guide to Benefit From Change, Profit From Failure, and Design Your Own Destiny! by Catherine Pulsifer

https://books2read.com/u/4D6vPk

Why not make your life what you deserve? It doesn't matter at what stage you are in life now, you can overcome debilitating obstacles that jeopardize your personal happiness, success and the destiny you deserve.

Here's what you'll learn:

- the two things that can dramatically change your life
- why some people are more successful than others
- how to defeat procrastination

- how to profit from failure

- the easiest way to change the world

- how to benefit from change

- plus much more.

MILLIONAIRE'S KEY HABITS FOR SUCCESS:

Adopt Their Attitudes To Create The Life You Want

by Byron Pulsifer

https://books2read.com/u/m2d9Q7

How do you achieve success?

Many years ago, if you had asked my parents to answer that question, they would have answered by saying that success depends on hard work. But what does that mean?

To answer that question, I thought about the many successful people I have encountered and read about. I categorized the key elements that stood out to me. My questions were simple. For example, what characteristics did they possess, and how did they use these characteristics to shape their success?

Let's face it; every person has faced disappointments, failures, and mistakes. So, how did they get beyond these?

Rarely, if ever, does one reach success with no challenges or issues. In this book, you will find the stories of people who have achieved success; you will discover the one key element they showed. And you will find suggestions about how to implement these elements in your life.

In addition, you will uncover the key underlying element that all the people discussed in this book have.

Success is not just one thing; it is a combination of things. But before you can apply distinct elements, and if you do not possess the underlying key for the foundation on which to start, then you end up with limited success.

THE CONFIDENCE GUIDE: 27 PROVEN WAYS TO BUILD YOUR SELF-WORTH

by Byron Pulsifer, Catherine Pulsifer

https://books2read.com/u/ml8kWB

What is self-worth? Why is it important?

Self-worth is a person's sense of their own worth, value, and positive regard for themselves. However, for many people, self-worth presents itself as a challenge, which can have serious physical and mental health consequences.

Why is having self-worth so vital?

- Understanding the importance of self-worth can help you have better relationships, both intimate and with friends.

- Self-worth helps people to be assertive and honest with themselves and others.

- It encourages healthy communication and the ability to speak up for your wants and needs without fear of judgment or criticism.

- When you have positive self-worth, your relationships will naturally follow suit, becoming happier, healthier, and more connected.

- Life can become an adventure that's full of possibility instead of seeing it as a succession of daunting tasks.

- Taking risks with optimism changes the entire landscape; rather than avoiding the unknown motivations that come from curiosity.

- Goals lead to achievement and failures become learning experiences.

- Instead of letting fear and negative self-talk hold you back, reclaiming your sense of self-worth allows you to become more confident in yourself, and this confidence allows you to open up and explore greater possibilities and opportunities for yourself.

Self-worth is a skill like any other, and you can learn how to do it if you know what steps to take and if you commit to putting in the effort. In this guide, you'll find everything you need to know about how to develop greater self-worth.

Reclaiming your sense of self-worth can be your life's game-changer.

Don't wait another day. Find out the 27 ways to help build your self-worth.

Also by Byron Pulsifer

The Road To Joy and Happiness How To: Develop Life-Changing Habits, Change Negative Behaviors, and Create The Life You Want
The Confidence Guide: 27 Proven Ways To Build Your Self-Worth

Watch for more at https://pulsiferbooks.com.

Also by Catherine Pulsifer

Wings

Wings for Work: Learn How To Develop and Use The Three Key Qualities That Successful People Have Mastered

Wings for Goals: How To Use Three Easy Steps to Change Your Life Forever!

Standalone

Millionaire's Key Habits for Success: Adopt Their Attitudes To Create The Life You Want

Wings of Wisdom: Your Daily Guide to Benefit from Change, Profit from Failure, and Design Your Own Destiny!

The Road To Joy and Happiness How To: Develop Life-Changing Habits, Change Negative Behaviors, and Create The Life You Want

The Confidence Guide: 27 Proven Ways To Build Your Self-Worth

Watch for more at https://pulsiferbooks.com.

About the Author

Byron Pulsifer

I have been fortunate enough to not only have received training in many facets of human behavior, but have also been able to use my training, skills, and experiences to engage in making life easier for many people.

Part of my experiences has included criminology, employee assistance, strategic planning, motivational seminars, small business ownership, and teaching essentials of the Christian faith.

I also firmly believe that learning never ends; it is an ongoing lifestyle that has framed how I approach each day of the year.

Catherine Pulsifer

I went from a high school secretarial graduate to a senior manager of a major international corporation. My employment advancement, however, was not without many hurdles that I had to overcome.

With many challenges facing me, at different times in my life, I was inspired by reading biographies of people who faced similar challenges, and by reading as many motivational and inspiring books as I could find.

I not only read these books but implemented the knowledge in my daily life, both personal and professional.

In 1998, I wrote my first book, "Wings of Wisdom". I was able to accomplish writing this book even though I had a demanding full-time job and two children at home. Part of my success in writing my first book was because I used the goal-setting strategies that I later wrote about in "Wings for Goals".

Since then, I have written additional books. "Wings for Work", focuses on issues in the workplace and how to develop and use three key qualities that helped me move forward in my professional life. And, my latest book, "Millionaire's Key Habits for Success", reveals the 9 key habits that millionaires used to secure their success.

I also devote a portion of my time to developing an inspirational and motivational website, www.stresslesscountry.com.

Read more at https://pulsiferbooks.com.

INSPIRATIONAL
PULSIFER BOOKS

About the Publisher

Pulsifer Books is dedicated to providing inspirational writings that apply to everyday life issues. These writings are filled with thoughts and strategies to help people move beyond where they are today to create a more balanced and rewarding lifestyle.

Pulsifer Books
https://pulsiferbooks.com

"After this manner pray ye:
Our Father which art in heaven,
Hollowed be thy name."
Matthew 6:9

WHEN YOU PRAY...
PRAY LIKE THIS

Dr. S. Walker

CONTENTS

DEDICATION

*This Devotional Study is Dedicated to
my grandson Isaiah,
who believes in the power of prayer*

*"Life is a journey that is traveled one day at a
time. No matter how well planned and equipped
we feel we are for it, life has its bumps in the road,
steep hills and mountains to climb and rivers to cross.
There is no alternative but to stay the journey with
self-confidence and optimism; accepting the cheering
and egging on by loved ones, but mostly embracing
the love of our Heavenly Father, keeping our hope
and faith in our Resurrected Lord Jesus Christ and
accepting the help and guidance of the Holy Spirit
all the while praying like this..."*

By Dr. Sheila Walker

Your purpose for this study:

_____

_____

_____

_____

_____

It happened that while Jesus was praying in a certain place,
after He had finished, one of His disciples said to Him,
"Lord, teach us to pray just as John also taught his disciples."
Luke 11:1

Your Personal Prayer Declaration:

_____

_____

_____

_____

_____

_____

_____

_____

_____

_____

_____

_____

_____

_____

Chapter One
An Explanation of Prayer

The first mention of prayer in the Bible is found in *Genesis 4:25-26,* "And Adam knew his wife again; and she bore a son, and called his name Seth: For God, hath appointed me another seed instead of Abel, whom Cain slew. And to Seth, to him also there was born a son; and he called his name Enos (Enoch): then began men to call upon the name of the LORD."

Abel, one of Adam and Eve's sons, was considered a "righteous man" because he offered God acceptable offerings. Cain, his brother who did not, killed Abel out of jealousy. The two brothers and their actions made the distinction between the "righteous" and the "unrighteous" generations that would follow.

After losing the "righteous" man in Abel, God replaced him with Seth, whose son Enoch, walked closely with God *(Read Genesis 5:24).* He spent quality time talking with Him and calling upon the name of the LORD. This is how prayer and public worship to God was introduced.

Hebrews 11:4 "By faith Abel brought God a better offering than Cain did. By faith he was commended as righteous, when God spoke well of his offerings. And by faith Abel still speaks, even though he is dead." New International Version

Genesis 4:8 "Now Cain said to his brother Abel, Let's go out to the field. While they were in the field, Cain attacked his brother Abel and killed him." New International Version

THE DIFFERENCE BETWEEN OLD AND NEW TESTAMENT PRAYERS:

The foundation of Old Testament prayers was based mostly on a covenant with God that was directed toward His character. Covenants are promises or agreements between God and His people, which were intended to consequent a dispensation *(a period of time that God tested man's obedience).*

The seven dispensations in Scripture *are:* Innocence *(Genesis 1:26),* Conscience *(Genesis 3:24),* Human Government *(Genesis*

8:20), Promise *(Genesis 12:1)*, Law *(Exodus 19:8)*, Grace *(John 1:17)* and the Kingdom *(Ephesians 1:10)*.

THE EIGHT COVENANTS IN SCRIPTURE ARE THE:

Edenic
Genesis 1:28 "And God blessed them, and God said unto them, Be fruitful, and multiply, and replenish the earth, and subdue it: and have dominion over the fish of the sea, and over the fowl of the air, and over every living thing that moveth upon the earth."

Adamic
Genesis 3:15 "And I will put enmity between thee and the woman, and between thy seed and her seed; it shall bruise thy head, and thou shalt bruise his heel."

Noahic
Genesis 9:15-17 "And I will remember My covenant, which is between Me and you and every living creature of all flesh; and never again shall the water become a flood to destroy all flesh. When the bow is in the cloud, then I will look upon it, to remember the everlasting covenant between God and every living creature of all flesh that is on the earth." And God said to Noah, "This is the sign of the covenant which I have established between Me and all flesh that is on the earth."

Abrahamic
Genesis 15:18 "In the same day the LORD made a covenant with Abram, saying, Unto thy seed have I given this land, from the river of Egypt unto the great river, the river Euphrates."

Moasic
Exodus 19:5-6 "Now then, if you will indeed obey My voice and keep My covenant, then you shall be My own possession among all the peoples, for all the earth is Mine; and you shall be to Me a kingdom of priests and a holy nation. These are the words that you shall speak to the sons of Israel." New American Standard Bible

Palestinian

Deuteronomy 30:1-3 "So it shall be when all of these things have come upon you, the blessing and the curse which I have set before you, and you call them to mind in all nations where the LORD your God has banished you, and you return to the LORD your God and obey Him with all your heart and soul according to all that I command you today, you and your sons, then the LORD your God will restore you from captivity, and have compassion on you, and will gather you again from all the peoples where the LORD your God has scattered you." New American Standard Bible

Davidic

2ⁿᵈ Samuel 7:16 "And thine house and thy kingdom shall be established for ever before thee: thy throne shall be established forever."

New

Hebrews 8:8 "For finding fault with them, he saith, Behold, the days come, saith the Lord, when I will make a new covenant with the house of Israel and with the house of Judah."

Although these prayers were heartfelt and sincere, they mostly address earthly needs and blessings. In the New Testament, prayers are more intimate because a personal relationship with God through Jesus Christ is developed. These prayers also address earthly needs with emphasis placed more on spiritual warfare, growth, faith and heavenly blessings.

OLD TESTAMENT PRAYER EXAMPLE:

Exodus 32:11-14 "And Moses besought the LORD his God, and said, LORD, why doth thy wrath wax hot against thy people, which thou hast brought forth out of the land of Egypt with great power, and with a mighty hand? Wherefore should the Egyptians speak, and say, For mischief did he bring them out, to slay them in the mountains, and to consume them from the face of the earth? Turn from thy fierce wrath, and repent of this evil against thy people. Remember Abraham, Isaac, and Israel *(Jacob before God changed his name in Genesis 35:10),* thy servants, to whom thou swarest by thine own self, and saidst unto them, I will multiply your seed as the stars of heaven, and all this land that I have spoken of will I give unto your seed, and they shall inherit *it* forever."

The Situation:
While Moses was away meeting with God to receive His commandments, the people he led out of Egypt quickly became impatient waiting for his return. They reverted to the religious practices of their oppressors and built a golden image to worship. This thing that they put in the place of God to worship made God angry enough to want to destroy them all.

The Need:
To turn away God's anger against the sinful actions of the people He delivered from bondage in Egypt.

The Prayer:
Moses, out of a sympathetic heart, pleaded for God's mercy by reminding Him of the promise He made to bless the seed of Abraham, Isaac and Jacob *(whose name was changed to Israel, the name they are called as a nation of people).*

New Testament Example of Prayer:

New Testament prayers illustrate a dependent, humble child who realizes that his need is more spiritual than natural. He needs the help and guidance from a strong, wise and loving heavenly Father.

Ephesians 6:12 "For we wrestle not against flesh and blood, but against principalities, against powers, against the rulers of the darkness of this world, against spiritual wickedness in high places."

Ephesians 1:3 "Praise be to the God and Father of our Lord Jesus Christ, who has blessed us in the heavenly realms with every spiritual blessing in Christ."

Our heavenly Father expects us to come to Him in prayer because it is His desire to meet the needs of His children with all spiritual blessings.

Hebrews 4:16 "Let us therefore come boldly unto the throne of grace, that we may obtain mercy, and find grace to help in time of need."

Matthew 7:11 "If ye then, being evil, know how to give good gifts unto your children, how much more shall your Father which is in heaven give good things to them that ask him?"

Chapter Two
God's View of Prayer

THEY ARE PRECIOUS

Our prayers are important to God; they are cherished and valued by Him.

Psalm 141:2 "Let my prayer be set forth before thee *as* incense; *and* the lifting up of my hands *as* the evening sacrifice."

David knowing how God felt about prayer and being far from a temple, wanted his sincere prayer to go up before God and be pleasing to Him. He wanted his prayer to remind God of the pleasure He finds in the aroma of sweet incense that was offered with the morning and evening Tabernacle sacrifices.

GOD'S PROMISE TO ANSWER OUR PRAYERS

2ⁿᵈ Chronicles 7:14 "If my people, which are called by my name, shall humble themselves, and pray, and seek my face, and turn from their wicked ways; then will I hear from heaven, and will forgive their sin, and will heal their land."

1ˢᵗ Kings 3:5 "In Gibeon, the LORD appeared to Solomon in a dream by night: and God said, "Ask what I shall give thee."

Isaiah 65:24 "And it shall come to pass, that before they call, I will answer; and while they are yet speaking, I will hear."

Psalm 91:15 "He shall call upon me, and I will answer him: I will *be* with him in trouble; I will deliver him, and honour him."

Jeremiah 33:3 "Call unto me, and I will answer thee, and shew thee great and mighty things, which thou knowest not."

GOD WANTS US TO ASK AND SEEK HIM

Deuteronomy 4:29 "But if from thence thou shalt seek the LORD thy God, thou shalt find *him*, if thou seek him with all thy heart and with all thy soul."

Luke 11:9 "And I say unto you, Ask, and it shall be given you; seek, and ye shall find; knock, and it shall be opened unto you."

Because God is omnipotent *(all-powerful)* and omniscient *(all-knowing)*, it is our human nature to inquire of Him; He has all of the answers to our questions concerning life, which is why we are encouraged to *ask:*

WITHOUT FEAR

Matthew 7:8 "For every one that asketh receiveth; and he that seeketh findeth; and to him that knocketh it shall be opened."

WITH OPENNESS

John 14:13 "And whatsoever ye shall ask in my name, that will I do, that the Father may be glorified in the Son."

HAVING FAITH

1st John 5:14 "And this is the confidence that we have in Him, that, if we ask any thing according to His will, He hears us."

BEING STABLE WITHOUT WAVERING

James 1:5-6 "If any of you lack wisdom, let him ask of God, that giveth to all men liberally, and upbraideth not; and it shall be given him. But let him ask in faith, nothing wavering. For he that wavers is like a wave of the sea driven with the wind and tossed."

WHILE DOING THE RIGHT THING

1st John 3: 22 "And whatever we ask, we receive of Him, because we keep His commandments, and do those things that are pleasing in His sight."

"When my soul fainted within me I remembered the LORD: and my prayer came in unto thee, into thine holy temple."
Jonah 2:7

Chapter Three
Jesus and Prayer

Christ being the Logos *("word" or expressions of God)* teaches us how to pray. He teaches that we should pray *without:*

HYPOCRISY

Matthew 6:5 "And when thou prayest, thou shalt not be as the hypocrites *are*: for they love to pray standing in the synagogues and in the corners of the streets, that they may be seen of men. Verily I say unto you, They have their reward."

SELF-RIGHTEOUSNESS

Luke 18:9-14 "And he spake also this parable unto certain who trusted in themselves that they were righteous, and set all others at naught? Two men went up into the temple to pray; the one a Pharisee, and the other a publican. The Pharisee stood and prayed thus with himself, God, I thank thee, that I am not as the rest of men, extortioners, unjust, adulterers, or even as this publican. I fast twice in the week; I give tithes of all that I get. But the publican, standing afar off, would not lift up so much as his eyes unto heaven, but smote his breast, saying, God, be thou merciful to me a sinner. I say unto you, This man went down to his house justified rather than the other: for every one that exalteth himself shall be humbled; but he that humbleth himself shall be exalted." American Standard Version

VAIN REPETITIONS

Matthew 6:7 "But when ye pray, use not vain repetitions, as the heathen *do*: for they think that they shall be heard for their much speaking."

UNFORGIVENESS

Matthew 6:14 "For if ye forgive men their trespasses, your heavenly Father will also forgive you."

UNBELIEF

Mark 11:24 "Therefore I say unto you, What things soever ye desire, when you pray, believe that ye receive them and ye shall have them."

PUBLIC DISPLAY

Matthew 6:6 "But thou, when thou prayest, enter into thy closet, and when thou hast shut thy door, pray to thy Father which is in secret; and thy Father which seeth in secret shall reward thee openly."

JESUS' MODELS FOR PRAYER ARE:

IN HIS NAME

John 14:13 "And whatsoever ye shall ask in my name, that will I do, that the Father may be glorified in the Son."

AGREEMENT IN SOCIAL PRAYER

Matthew 18:19 "Again I say unto you, That if two of you shall agree on earth as touching anything that they shall ask, it shall be done for them of my Father which is in heaven."

JOHN 17 PRAYER – Included Prayer *for:*

HIMSELF – that His ministry work would glorify the Father.

John 17:1-5 "These words spake Jesus, and lifted up his eyes to heaven, and said, Father, the hour is come; glorify thy Son, that thy Son also may glorify thee: As thou hast given him power over all flesh, that he should give eternal life to as many as thou hast given him. And this is life eternal, that they might know thee the only true God, and Jesus Christ, whom thou hast sent. I have glorified thee on the earth: I have finished the work which thou gavest me to do. And now, O Father, glorify thou me with thine own self with the glory which I had with thee before the world was."

HIS DISCIPLES

John 17:6-19 "I have manifested thy name unto the men which thou gavest me out of the world: thine they were, and thou gavest them me; and they have kept thy word. Now they have known that all things whatsoever thou hast given me are of thee. For I have given unto them the words which thou gavest me; and they have received *them*, and have known surely that I came out from thee, and they have believed that thou didst send me. I pray for them: I pray not for the world, but for them which thou hast given me; for they are thine. And all mine are thine, and thine are mine; and I am glorified in them. And now I am no more in the world, but these are in the world, and I come to thee. Holy Father, keep through thine own name those whom thou hast given me, that they may be one, as we *are*. While I was with them in the world, I kept them in thy name: those that thou gavest me I have kept, and none of them is lost, but the son of perdition; that the scripture might be fulfilled. And now come I to thee; and these things I speak in the world, that they might have my joy fulfilled in themselves. I have given them thy word; and the world hath hated them, because they are not of the world, even as I am not of the world. I pray not that thou shouldest take them out of the world, but that thou shouldest keep them from the evil. They are not of the world, even as I am not of the world. Sanctify them through thy truth: thy word is truth. As thou hast sent me into the world, even so have I also sent them into the world. And for their sakes I sanctify myself, that they also might be sanctified through the truth."

ALL BELIEVERS

John 17:20-26 "Neither pray I for these alone, but for them also which shall believe on me through their word; That they all may be one; as thou, Father, *art* in me, and I in thee, that they also may be one in us: that the world may believe that thou hast sent me. And the glory which thou gavest me I have given them; that they may be one, even as we are one: I in them, and thou in me, that they may be made perfect in one; and that the world may know that thou hast sent me, and hast loved them, as thou hast loved me. Father, I will that they also, whom thou hast given me, be with me where I am; that they may behold my glory, which thou hast given me: for thou lovedst me before the foundation of the world. O righteous Father, the world hath not known thee: but I have known thee, and these have known that thou hast sent me. And I have declared unto them thy name, and will declare it: that the love wherewith thou hast loved me may be in them, and I in them."

THE LORD'S PRAYER

PRAISE TO THE FATHER

Matthew 6:9 "After this manner therefore pray ye: Our Father which art in heaven, Hallowed be thy name."

THE AUTHORITY OF GOD

Matthew 6:10 "Thy kingdom come. Thy will be done in earth, as *it is* in heaven."

DAILY PROVISION

Matthew 6:11 "Give us this day our daily bread."

FORGIVENESS

Matthew 6:12 "And forgive us our debts, as we forgive our debtors."

DELIVERANCE FROM TEMPTATIONS AND ACKNOWLEDGEMENT OF GOD'S POWER

Matthew 6:13 "And lead us not into temptation, but deliver us from evil: For thine is the kingdom, and the power, and the glory, forever. Amen."

OTHER EXAMPLES OF CHRIST'S PRAYERS

AT THE END OF THE DAY

Matthew 14:23 "And when he had sent the multitudes away, he went up into a mountain apart to pray: and when the evening was come, he was there alone."

OVER FOOD

Matthew 15:36 "And he took the seven loaves and the fishes, and gave thanks, and break them, and gave to his disciples, and the disciples to the multitude."

IN THE WILDERNESS

Luke 5:15-16 "But so much the more went there a fame abroad of him: and great multitudes came together to hear, and to be healed by him of their infirmities. And he withdrew himself into the wilderness, and prayed."

IN DISTRESS

John 12:27 "Now is my soul troubled; and what shall I say? Father, save me from this hour: but for this cause came I unto this hour."

FOR THE COMFORTER TO COME

John 14:16-17 "And I will pray the Father, and He shall give you another Comforter, that he may abide with you forever; Even the Spirit of truth; whom the world cannot receive, because it seeth Him not, neither knoweth Him: but ye know Him; for He dwelleth with you, and shall be in you."

IN SORROW

Matthew 26:26-28 "Then cometh Jesus with them unto a place called Gethsemane, and saith unto the disciples, Sit ye here, while I go and pray yonder. And He took with Him Peter and the two sons of Zebedee, and began to be sorrowful and very heavy. Then saith He unto them, My soul is exceedingly sorrowful, even unto death: tarry ye here, and watch with me."

FOR PETER

Luke 22:31-32 "And the Lord said, Simon, Simon, behold, Satan hath desired to have you, that he may sift you as wheat: But I have prayed for thee, that thy faith fail not: and when thou art converted, strengthen thy brethren."

Chapter Four
Important Elements of Prayer

WORSHIP

To Worship God means to pay respect, reverence, submit, show love, adoration and esteem Him very greatly.

Worship is first and foremost at the beginning of prayer because it acknowledges the spiritual realm of God that we are entering into. It also shows our willingness to yield ourselves to His domain.

Matthew 6:9-10 "After this manner therefore, pray ye: Our Father which art in heaven, Hallowed be thy name. Thy kingdom come, Thy will be done in earth, as it is in heaven."

Psalm 95:1-2 "O come, let us sing unto the LORD: let us make a joyful noise to the rock of our salvation. Let us come before his presence with thanksgiving, and make a joyful noise unto him with psalms."

CONFESSION [1]

After acknowledging Him, we should talk about ourselves by confessing our sins, shortcomings, disobedience and the grief we feel because of it. This part of prayer is so personally convicting, that it has the tendency to be omitted. To not confess our faults is, in and of itself, a sin because it suggests that we are equal to God, who is sinless.

Romans 3:23 "For all have sinned and come short of the Glory of God."

James 5:16 "Confess your faults one to another, and pray one for another, that ye may be healed. The effectual *(powerful, able)* fervent prayer *(passionate, truthful)* of a righteous *(honest, upright)* man availeth much."

Psalm 139:23-24 "Search me, O God, and know my heart; test me and know my anxious thoughts. See if there is any offensive way in me, and lead me in the way everlasting." New International Version

1st John 1:9 "If we confess our sins, he is faithful and just to forgive us our sins, and to cleanse us from all unrighteousness."

COMMON SINS COMMITTED BY CHRISTIANS

As Christians, living in the progressive stage of sanctification, we make mistakes and can at times displease God. Thankfully, we have the help of the Holy Spirit living within us to make us aware of our wrong by "convicting" us. Because we do not practice sin, nor live in the "state" of sin, we should never ignore the Holy Spirit when He reveals our faults and prompts us to confess them.

Sins of the Body:

- THE EYE – things we gaze at that causes want, greed, lust or criticism of others
- OMISSION – excluding or leaving something out
- HEARING AMISS – hearing incorrectly, invalidly or speciously
- GOSSIP – spreading rumors, scandal, hearsay
- SLOTHFULNESS – laziness or idleness
- PROCRASTINATION – deferment or putting off, stalling

Sins of the Mind:

- DOUBT – distrust, disbelief, suspicion
- FALSE PREDICTIONS – fearful anticipations or hopes, outcome
- CARNAL THINKING – fleshly mindset
- NEGATIVITY – thinking and/or speaking negativity or unconstructively
- VAIN IMAGINATION – futile ingenuity or vision, vanity of the mind

- PRIDE – arrogance or conceit

Sins of the Heart:

- ABANDONMENT – feelings of being rejected, neglected or forgotten by God

- JEALOUSY – being envious or resentful of someone else

- UN-FORGIVENESS – inability to forgive or extend grace

- FEAR – frightening thoughts or ideas, feeling apprehensive or anxious

- WORRIEDNESS – being fearful, nervous, alarmed or disquieted

- STUBBORNNESS – willfulness, inflexibility or being uncooperative

- SELF-RIGHTEOUSNESS – pomposity or sanctimoniousness

ACCEPTING GOD'S WILL

Acceptance of God's Will is to have faith in His desire, purpose or Divine predetermination concerning us. This trust is based on our relationship with Him as our heavenly Father who knows our future. Acknowledging God's Will when we pray is not only a confession of trust and faith, but our willingness to be obedient as well.

Proverbs 3:5-6 "Trust in the LORD with all thine heart; and lean not unto thine own understanding. In all thy ways acknowledge him, and he shall direct thy paths."

When we pray asking that God's Will be done, we must keep in mind that the answer might not be what we expect it to be. Whatever His answer is, it is His desire or purpose for us at that time; therefore, we should be satisfied.

EXAMPLE – "YES" TO THE LEPER'S PRAYER

Luke 5:12 "And it came to pass, when he was in a certain city, behold a man full of leprosy: who seeing Jesus fell on *his* face, and besought him, saying, Lord, if thou wilt, thou canst make me clean. And he put forth his hand, and touched him, saying, I will: be clean. And immediately the leprosy departed from him."

EXAMPLE – "NO" TO JESUS' PRAYER SO THAT DIVINE PURPOSE WOULD BE FULFILLED

Matthew 26:39 "And he went a little farther, and fell on his face, and prayed, saying, O my Father, if it be possible, let this cup pass from me: nevertheless not as I will, but as you will."

Jesus' prayer request was not to change the Father's purpose for His life. Jesus knew, understood and spoke often of His purpose, which was to bring salvation to mankind. The physical torture and pain involved in fulfilling that purpose was what weighed heavily on Jesus' heart. But even to that impending agony, He subjected His own will to that of His Father's.

EXAMPLE – "MORE" THAN WHAT YOU ASKED FOR

1ˢᵗ Kings 3:7-14 (Solomon's Prayer: vs. 7-9) "Now, O LORD my God, You have made Your servant king in place of my father David, yet I am but a little child; I do not know how to go out or come in. Your servant is in the midst of Your people which You have chosen, a great people who are too many to be numbered or counted. So give Your servant an understanding heart to judge Your people to discern between good and evil. For who is able to judge this great people of Yours?" *(God's Answer: vs. 10-14)* "It was pleasing in the sight of the Lord that Solomon had asked this thing. God said to him, Because you have asked this thing and have not asked for yourself long life, nor have asked riches for yourself, nor have you asked for the life of your enemies, but have asked for yourself discernment to understand justice, behold, I have done according to your words. Behold, I have given you a wise and discerning heart, so that there has been no one like you before you, nor shall one like you arise after you. I have also given you what you have not asked, both riches and honor, so that there will not be any among the kings like you all your days. If you walk in My ways, keeping My statutes and commandments, as your father David walked, then I will prolong your days." New American Standard Bible

Solomon, who asked for wisdom rather than riches, was given the wisdom he asked for with the addition of more riches, honor and longer life.

Acts 12:5-14 (The Church Praying) "Peter therefore was kept in prison: but prayer was made without ceasing of the church unto God for him." *(God's answer in Acts 12:12-14)* "And when he had considered the thing, he came to the house of Mary the mother of John, whose surname was Mark; where many were gathered together praying. And as Peter knocked at the door of the gate, a damsel came to hearken, named Rhoda. And when she knew Peter's voice, she opened not the gate for gladness, but ran in, and told how Peter stood before the gate."

The church prayed concerning Peter's arrest and pending trial, God answered them with his miraculous freedom.

EXAMPLE – "INSTEAD OF" AS AN ANSWER TO PRAYER

2ⁿᵈ Corinthians 12:7-10 "And by reason of the exceeding greatness of the revelations, that I should not be exalted overmuch, there was given to me a thorn in the flesh, a messenger of Satan to buffet me, that I should not be exalted overmuch. Concerning this thing I besought the Lord thrice, that it might depart from me. And he hath said unto me, My grace is sufficient for thee: for my power is made perfect in weakness. Most gladly therefore will I rather glory in my weaknesses, that the power of Christ may rest upon me. Wherefore I take pleasure in weakness, in injuries, in necessities, in persecutions, in distresses, for Christ's sake: for when for when I am weak, then am I strong."

Rather than heal Paul of the issue that caused him pain and discomfort, the Lord blessed him with His Grace and Power which brought glory to Him through Paul's life. Paul gladly accepted God's answer and saw it as a way to be humbled and strengthened.

SINCERITY: [2]

Prayer should never be an exercise to show how religious we are. Nor should it be a psychological activity that we perform to convince ourselves that we have the ability to change God's will for us. These would be considered hypocritical or self-righteous prayers. We should always pray that God's will be done in our lives.

James 4:3 "Ye ask, and receive not, because ye ask amiss *(wrong motives, inappropriately),* that ye may consume *(utilize or use)* it upon your lusts *(your own pleasure)*."

Matthew 6:6-7 "But thou, when thou prayest, enter into thy closet, and when thou hast shut thy door, pray to thy Father which is in secret; and thy Father which seeth in secret shall reward thee openly. But when ye pray, use not vain repetitions, as the heathen do: for they think that they shall be heard for their much speaking."

"At that time Jesus answered and said, I thank thee,
O Father, Lord of heaven and earth."
Matthew 11:25

Chapter Five
Prayer Problems

As with everything else in life, there are problems associated with prayer. These problems exist because prayer is a personal spiritual phenomenon. Communicating with God through prayer has many facets that require practice over a period of time. Prayer is private and particular to the individual and, as a result, personality and behavior can interfere, thus causing problems with effectiveness. Listed below are the most common prayer problems with solutions to help maintain a strong, consistent prayer life.

PROBLEM – INDIFFERENCE: having a neutral attitude, a lack of sincerity or seeming disinterested in the prayer.

Isaiah 32:9 "Rise up, you women who are at ease, hear my voice; you complacent daughters, give ear to my speech." English Standard Version

SOLUTION:

Remember that prayer is necessary at all times. Understand that prayer is how we:

- Communicate with God
- Foster a good relationship with the Father
- Strengthen our faith and trust in God
- Learn of God's Will for us
- Confuse Satan and ward off the powers of darkness

PROBLEM – PERSONAL INDIFFERENCE: conforming to a state or condition which makes fervency in prayer unnecessary because everything seems to be okay.

SOLUTIONS:

- Force yourself out of that attitude by becoming enthusiastic about the other good things God wants for you
- Recite the Scriptures of His plans and promises for your life

- Become interested in your future and what you're believing God for

PROBLEM – INSTABILITY IN PRAYER: wavering or not being sure about believing God for an answer.

James 1:6-7 "But let him ask in faith, nothing wavering. For he that wavereth is like a wave of the sea driven with the wind and tossed. For let not that man think that he shall receive any thing of the Lord. A double minded man *is* unstable in all his ways."

SOLUTION:

A "double minded" man refers to a person that has two "souls" within him. He speaks with one soul but acts with the other. A stable prayer is a prayer that is spoken without contradicting action.

PROBLEM – SELF-INDULGENT PRAYER: unwise prayers based on personal desires and pleasures.

James 4:3 "And even when you ask, you don't get it because your motives are all wrong – you want only what will give you pleasure." New Living Translation

SOLUTION:

How to solve this type of prayer problem is within the scripture itself ... "wrong motives." God wants to give us the desires of our hearts, prosperity and the goodness of life. However, we should want more of His Divine Will for us which includes a closer relationship with Him, good health and a peaceful and contented life. Adding to this would be His Will for our families, friends, neighbors, leaders, world peace and the betterment of all mankind.

PROBLEM – LACK OF UNITY IN PRAYER: not asking for the same outcome when praying with other people or in a group is a serious problem. Lack of unity can hinder or delay an answer to prayer; which makes unity in prayer very important.

SOLUTION:

When praying with an individual or praying with a group, knowing the reason and desired outcome of the prayer should be clearly understood. This will ensure that everyone is praying and believing God for the same thing.

In this practice, we should be careful not to give God instructions on how to provide blessings and deliverance. Remember that He is a sovereign God, no one knows His mind and He cannot be counseled. Just as Jesus prayed that the Will of the Father be done, so should we.

Examples of the Power of Unity in Prayer

Matthew 18:19 "Again I say unto you, That if two of you shall agree on earth as touching anything that they shall ask, it shall be done for them of my Father which is in heaven."

Notice: Agreement

Acts: 1:14 "They all joined together constantly in prayer, along with the women and Mary the mother of Jesus, and with his brothers." New International Version

Notice: Continued prayer with one accord and supplication

Acts: 4:24 "And when they heard it, they lifted their voices together to God and said, "Sovereign Lord, who made the heaven and the earth and the sea and everything in them." English Standard Version

Notice: They lifted up their voices to God together, meaning one prayer not many different prayers

Acts: 12:5 "Peter therefore was kept in prison: but prayer was made without ceasing of the church unto God for him."

Notice: While Peter was in jail, the church prayed together for one thing concerning him. They were so persistent; they didn't realize that they'd gotten their answer. *(Read verses 6-15)*

SUCCESS IN PRAYER

REPENTANCE – having a contrite *(sorrowful)* spirit.

WHOLE HEARTINESS – not being divided in the intent of the heart, to have the right motive, to be truthful and sincere.

James 4:3 "When you ask, you do not receive, because you ask with wrong motives, that you may spend what you get on your pleasures." New International Version

FAITH – accepting God's Will as an absolute for your life, even if it seems intangible or vague.

Hebrews 11:1 "Now faith is the substance of things hoped for, the evidence of things not seen."

RIGHTEOUSNESS – being upright and honorable in your daily walk with Christ.

James 5:16 "Confess *your* faults one to another, and pray one for another, that ye may be healed. The effectual fervent prayer of a righteous man availeth much."

OBEDIENCE – follow the instructions of God even if it seems difficult.

1ˢᵗ John 3:22 "And whatsoever we ask, we receive of him, because we keep his commandments, and do those things that are pleasing in his sight."

Knowing the problems associated with prayer and practicing their solutions will help to develop a more successful prayer life. We should be assured that our Father will answer our prayers according to His Divine Will and in His perfect timing.

Psalm 91:15 "He shall call upon me, and I will answer him."

Isaiah 58:9 "then shalt thou call and the Lord shall answer; thou shalt cry, and He sall say, here I am."

31

Isaiah 65:24 "And it shall come to pass, that before they call, I will answer; and while they are yet speaking, I will hear."

Chapter Six
Waiting on the Lord

Isaiah 40:29-31 "He gives power to the faint; and to them that have no might he increases strength *(God's provision)*. Even the youths shall faint and be weary, and the young men shall utterly fall: *(Everyone experiences times of faintheartedness)*. But they that wait on the LORD shall renew their strength; they shall mount up with wings as eagles *(a metaphor for strength)*; they shall run, and not be weary; and they shall walk, and not faint *(God's best is the outcome of your patient wait)*." American King James Version

WHAT WAITING MEANS

"To Wait on the Lord" means to remain calm and take no action upon yourself because you are expecting *(with enthusiasm)* a divine outcome to your prayer. It also means that you are receiving peace and seeking divine counseling during this time. This explains why you continue to wait on God even when you are tempted to do something on your own.

Waiting also proves that you are obedient. At times you may feel the urge to take matters into your own hands, but you don't; that is because you realize that God has placed restraints on you for that period of time. You resist impulsive decisions to avoid being out of God's perfect Divine Will. Your waiting proves that you trust God more than your own feelings.

WHAT WAITING DOES NOT MEAN

Waiting on God does not imply that you do absolutely nothing. While waiting on God, you should be *active:*

1. Building your character so that you develop and increase the virtue of patience.

2. Increasing your prayer life so that you stay in close communication with God to keep you encouraged as you wait.

3. Noticing the subtle moves of God and events in your life that progress you towards the answer to your prayer.

4. With other commitments which serve as healthy diversions that

will keep you occupied as you wait for answers to your situation. Revisit unfinished projects, gifts and talents that you've put on the back burner. This is a good time to take your focus off your present situation and put positive energy into those things that have been neglected or postponed.

The feeling of non-progression or having your life seem as though it's on hold happens to everyone. Because life is a series of occasions that can provoke making serious decisions and choices, you can become overwhelmed and weary; which leads to emotional distress. However, you should continue to *wait:*

- So that you don't make hasty decisions
- Knowing that God is with you
- For spiritual renewal and strength from God
- Understanding that in your waiting there is spiritual progress
- Being assured that the end result will be beneficial to you

1st Chronicles 29:12 "Both riches and honour come of Thee, and thou reignest over all; and in thine hands is the power and might; and in thine hand it is to make great, *(the power, might and sovereignty of God who is our source of strength)* and to give strength unto all."

Psalm 46:1 "God is our refuge and strength, a very present *(there at all times)* help in trouble."

Psalm 73:26 "My flesh and my heart faileth: but God is the strength of my heart, and my portion *(God is the quantity or extent of my life)* forever."

STUDY VERSES ON PATIENCE AND WAITING ON THE LORD:

Ecclesiastes 7:8 "Better is the end of a thing than the beginning thereof; and the patient in spirit *(the trusting and obedient spirit)* is better than the proud in spirit."

Romans 12:12 "Rejoicing in hope; patient in tribulation; continuing instant in prayer (a consistent prayer life)."

Hebrews 10:36 "For ye have need of patience, that, after ye have done the will of God *(after you have waited)*, ye might *(be able to)* receive the promise."

Psalm 37:7 "Rest in the Lord, and wait patiently for him; fret not thyself because of him who prospereth in his way *(those who seem to be progressing beyond you)*, because of the man who bringeth wicked devices to pass *(they are operating on their own and probably will not last)*."

Psalm 40:1 "I waited patiently for the Lord; and he inclined *(leaned toward or favored)* unto me, and heard my cry."

Chapter Seven
Persistence in Prayer

Persistent prayers are prayers of faith that are prayed in times of desperation. These are prayers we pray for our own personal needs or on behalf of someone else until they are answered. This type of prayer should not be considered repetitious prayers. The reason being, as we see portions answered the prayer changes to focus on what remains unanswered. This is called "praying through."

Praise and thankfulness is given throughout the duration of the request because it is a progressive prayer with expectation and hope until it is completely answered. Study the following prayers in your Bible to learn how each prayer was answered. Notice that regardless to how discouraging a favorable answer may have seemed, those praying were persistent.

JACOB WRESTLING WITH GOD

Genesis 32:25-26 "And when he saw that he prevailed not against him, he touched the hollow of his thigh; and the hollow of Jacob's thigh was out of joint, as he wrestled with him. And he said, Let me go, for the day breaketh. And he said, I will not let thee go, except thou bless me."

THE SYROPHENICIAN WOMAN

Matthew 15:23-27 "And, behold, a woman of Canaan came out of the same coasts, and cried unto Him, saying, Have mercy on me, O Lord, thou Son of David; my daughter is grievously vexed with a devil. But He answered her not a word. And His disciples came and besought Him, saying, Send her away; for she crieth after us. But He answered and said, I am not sent but unto the lost sheep of the house of Israel. Then came she and worshipped Him, saying, Lord, help me. But He answered and said, It is not meet to take the children's bread, and to cast it to dogs. And she said, Truth, Lord: yet the dogs eat of the crumbs which fall from their masters' table."

JESUS FACING HIS BIGGEST TRIAL

Luke 22:44 "And being in agony he prayed more earnestly: and his sweat was as it were great drops of blood falling down to the ground."

THE NOBLEMAN FROM CAPERNAUM

John 4:46-49 "Once more He visited Cana in Galilee, where He had turned the water into wine. And there was a certain royal official whose son lay sick at Capernaum. When this man heard that Jesus had arrived in Galilee from Judea, he went to Him and begged Him to come and heal his son, who was close to death. Unless you people see signs and wonders, Jesus told him, you will never believe. The royal official said, Sir, come down before my child dies." New International Version

"And Hezekiah prayed before the LORD"
2ⁿᵈ Kings 19:15

"And Hezekiah prayed before the LORD"
2nd *Kings 19:15*

Chapter Eight
Prayers that Avail

Prayers that "avail" have an advantage because they are regulated by these Biblical principles of prayer:

CONFESSION

Psalm 66:18 "If I regard iniquity in my heart, the Lord will not hear me."

A HEART THAT FORGIVES [3] – Not being able to forgive is another hindrance to our prayers. When we refuse to forgive we stabilize a blockage between God and ourselves. If we have a problem with forgiving, we should ask for His help. Forgiveness plays a very important role in getting our prayers answered.

Mark 11:25-26 "And when you stand praying, forgive, if you have anything against any: that your Father also who is in heaven may forgive you your trespasses."

Matthew 6:15 "But if you do not forgive others their sins, your Father will not forgive your sins." New International Version

RIGHT MOTIVES – prayers that have adverse motives are easily recognized by our heart and conscious.

James 4:3 "You ask for something but do not get it because you ask for it for the wrong reason for your own pleasure."

FAITH – more than believing; having trust in God

Hebrews 11:6 "And it is impossible to please God without faith. Anyone who wants to come to Him must believe that God exists and that He rewards those who sincerely seek Him."

GUIDANCE OF THE HOLY SPIRIT – as you are praying you may feel the urge to pray for something else that is pressing on your heart; this is one way to recognize that the Holy Spirit is guiding your prayer.

Romans 8:26-27 "In the same way, the Spirit helps us in our weakness. We do not know what we ought to pray for, but the Spirit himself intercedes for us with groans that words cannot express. And He who searches our hearts knows the mind of the Spirit, because the Spirit intercedes for the saints in accordance with God's will."

WITHIN THE WILL OF GOD – *(see Accepting God's Will page 22)*

1st John 5:14 "This is the confidence we have in approaching God: that if we ask anything according to His will, He hears us."

IN THE NAME OF JESUS [4] – Jesus is the gateway to the Father because of His death, burial and resurrection. His position is now in Heaven where He is seated on the right hand of the Father making intercession for us. Therefore, we should end our prayers by saying "In the name of Jesus, Amen *(truly, or let it be).*"

John 14:13 "And I will do whatever you ask in my name, so that the Son may bring glory *(praise, credit)* to the Father."

In addition, we must always remember to include reverence, worship, praise and adoration of The Father to our prayers to make them more meaningful.

"Lord, hear my voice. Let your ears be attentive to my cry for mercy."
Psalm 130:2

Chapter Nine
Fasting

Fasting is a highly spiritual and very personal religious activity that has several beneficial results. For example, fasting brings us closer to God, it helps us to discern and think more spiritually so that we make right choices during times of uncertainty. When we fast we become submissive to the Will of God and by fasting, we weaken ourselves so that we are strengthened by Him.

The Bible gives many other reasons why Christians should fast, but only gives these few rules to follow during a *fast:*

ALWAYS KEEP IN MIND GOD'S TRUE FAST FOR EVERY CHRISTIAN

Isaiah 58:5-11 "You humble yourselves by going through the motions of penance, bowing your heads like reeds bending in the wind. You dress in burlap and cover yourselves with ashes. Is this what you call fasting? Do you really think this will please the LORD? No, this is the kind of fasting I want: Free those who are wrongly imprisoned; lighten the burden of those who work for you. Let the oppressed go free, and remove the chains that bind people. Share your food with the hungry, and give shelter to the homeless. Give clothes to those who need them, and do not hide from relatives who need your help. Then your salvation will come like the dawn, and your wounds will quickly heal. Your godliness will lead you forward, and the glory of the LORD will protect you from behind. Then when you call, the LORD will answer. 'Yes, I am here,' He will quickly reply. Remove the heavy yoke of oppression. Stop pointing your finger and spreading vicious rumors! Feed the hungry, and help those in trouble. Then your light will shine out from the darkness, and the darkness around you will be as bright as noon. The LORD will guide you continually, giving you water when you are dry and restoring your strength. You will be like a well-watered garden, like an ever-flowing spring." New Living Translation

KEEP THIS SACRED ACT PRIVATE

Matthew 6:16-18 "Whenever you fast, do not put on a gloomy face as the hypocrites do, for they neglect their appearance so that they will be noticed by men when they are fasting. Truly I say to you, they have their reward in full. But you, when you fast, anoint your head and wash your face so that your fasting will not be noticed by men, but by your Father who is in secret; and your Father who sees what is done in secret will reward you." New American Standard Bible

DO NOT USE FASTING TO PERSUADE GOD

2nd Samuel 12:13 "And David said unto Nathan, I have sinned against the LORD. And Nathan said unto David, The LORD also hath put away thy sin; thou shalt not die. Howbeit, because by this deed thou hast given great occasion to the enemies of the LORD to blaspheme, the child also that is born unto thee shall surely die. And Nathan departed unto his house. And the LORD struck the child that Uriah's wife bare unto David, and it was very sick. David therefore besought God for the child; and David fasted, and went in, and lay all night upon the earth. And the elders of his house arose, and went to him, to raise him up from the earth: but he would not, neither did he eat bread with them. And it came to pass on the seventh day, that the child died. And the servants of David feared to tell him that the child was dead: for they said, Behold, while the child was yet alive, we spake unto him, and he would not hearken unto our voice: how will he then vex himself, if we tell him that the child is dead?"

OTHER REASONS TO FAST

DIVINE GUIDANCE

Judges 20:24-26 "And the children of Israel came near against the children of Benjamin the second day. And Benjamin went forth against them out of Gibeah the second day, and destroyed down to the ground of the children of Israel again eighteen thousand men; all these drew the sword. Then all the children of Israel, and all the people, went up, and came unto the house of God, and wept, and sat there before the LORD, and fasted that day until even, and offered burnt offerings and peace offerings before the LORD."

VICTORY OVER TEMPTATION

Matthew 4:1-4 "Then was Jesus led up of the Spirit into the wilderness to be tempted of the devil. And when He had fasted forty days and forty nights, He was afterward an hungred. And when the tempter came to Him, he said, If thou be the Son of God, command that these stones be made bread. But He answered and said, It is written, Man shall not live by bread alone, but by every word that proceedeth out of the mouth of God."

HUMILITY

Psalms 35:13 "They repay me evil for good and leave me like one bereaved. Yet when they were ill, I put on sackcloth and humbled myself with fasting. When my prayers returned to me unanswered, I went about mourning as though for my friend or brother. I bowed my head in grief as though weeping for my mother." New International Version

DELIVERANCE FROM DANGER

Acts 27:33 "And while the day was coming on, Paul besought them all to take meat, saying, This day is the fourteenth day that ye have tarried and continued fasting, having taken nothing. Wherefore I pray you to take some meat: for this is for your health: for there shall not an hair fall from the head of any of you."

MERCY

Jonah 3:4-10 "Then Jonah began to go through the city one day's walk; and he cried out and said, Yet forty days and Nineveh will be overthrown. Then the people of Nineveh believed in God; and they called a fast and put on sackcloth from the greatest to the least of them. When the word reached the king of Nineveh, he arose from his throne, laid aside his robe from him, covered himself with sackcloth and sat on the ashes. He issued a proclamation and it said, In Nineveh by the decree of the king and his nobles: Do not let man, beast, herd, or flock taste a thing. Do not let them eat or drink water. But both man and beast must be covered with sackcloth; and let men call on God earnestly that each may turn from his wicked way and from the violence which is in his hands. Who knows, God may turn and relent and withdraw His burning anger so that we will not perish. When God saw their deeds, that they turned from their wicked way, then God relented concerning the calamity which He had declared He would bring upon them. And He did not do it." New American Standard Bible

INSTRUCTIONS FROM GOD

Acts 13:2 "While they were worshiping the Lord and fasting, the Holy Spirit said, Set apart for me Barnabas and Saul for the work to which I have called them." English Standard Version

ON BEHALF OF SOMEONE ELSE

Esther 4:16 "Go and gather together all the Jews of Susa and fast for me. Do not eat or drink for three days, night or day. My maids and I will do the same. And then, though it is against the law, I will go in to see the king. If I must die, I must die."

A COMMON CAUSE

Joel 2:15-17 "Blow the ram's horn in Jerusalem! Announce a time of fasting; call the people together for a solemn meeting. Gather all the people, the elders, the children, and even the babies. Call the bridegroom from his quarters and the bride from her private room. Let the priests, who minister in the LORD's presence, stand and weep between the entry room to the Temple and the altar. Let them pray, Spare your people, LORD! Don't let your special possession become an object of mockery. Don't let them become a joke for unbelieving foreigners who say, Has the God of Israel left them?" New Living Translation

WHEN YOU FAST YOU SHOULD ALWAYS INCLUDE:

1. Prayer *(extremely necessary throughout the duration of the fast)*

2. Confession *(admission of wrong doing, which everyone is guilty of)* Romans 3:23

3. Repentance *(show regret with a contrition)*

Types of Fasting

The Absolute Fast
No food or drink *(if not possible, drink during the day)*.

The Partial Fast
Omitting certain meals, daily leisure or setting a particular time during the day.

Daniel Fast
No meat, bread or sweets, only bland vegetables.

Chapter Ten
Meditation

Meditation is a part of prayer that sadly is not practiced enough by today's Christians. This is unfortunate because *mediation:*

- Fosters our relationship with the Father

- Helps to strengthen our faith

- Provides us with spiritual benefits

- Guides our daily Christian walk

DEFINITIONS

WEBSTER – 1. (*n.*) The act of the mind in considering with attention; continued attention of the mind to a particular subject; meditation; musing; study.

2. (n.) Holy meditation.
3. (n.) The act of looking forward to an event as about to happen; expectation; the act of intending or purposing. Webster's Revised Unabridged Dictionary

HEBREW – siach *(see'-akh)* (verb) meaning to: muse, speak of, moan, sing

Psalm 143:5 "I remember the days of old; I meditate on all Your doings; I muse on the work of Your hands." New American Standard Bible

Psalm 77:12 "I will meditate also of all thy work, and talk of thy doings."

Psalm 19:14 "Let the words of my mouth, and the meditation of my heart, be acceptable in thy sight, O LORD, my strength, and my redeemer."

GREEK – *1)* promeletaó *(prom-el-et-ah'-o)* meaning to premeditate, prepare beforehand.

Luke 12:11-12 "And when they bring you unto the syna-gogues, and unto magistrates, and powers, take ye no thought how or what thing ye shall answer, or what ye shall say: For the Holy

Ghost shall teach you in the same hour what ye ought to say." In this example, Jesus instructs His disciples not to premeditate how they will answer Synagogue magistrates if they are brought to trial for witnessing.

2) enthumeomai *(en-thoo-meh'-om-ahee)* meaning to reflect on, to ponder.

Psalm 63:6 "When I remember thee upon my bed, *and* meditate on thee in the *night* watches."

Meditation is a vocal *(or sometimes silent)* part of prayer that reflects on the instructions, promises, blessings and provisions given to us in God's Word. Although mentioned mostly in the Old Testament *(primarily the Psalms)* examples of meditation are found in both Testaments.

MEDITATION *IS:*

ENCOURAGED IN THE WORD OF GOD

Psalm 1:1-2 "Blessed *is* the man that walketh not in the counsel of the ungodly, nor standeth in the way of sinners, nor sitteth in the seat of the scornful. But his delight is in the law of the LORD; and in His law doth he meditate day and night."

A SOURCE OF HOPE

Psalm 139:17-18 "How precious also are thy thoughts unto me, O God! how great is the sum of them! If I should count them, they are more in number than the sand: when I awake, I am still with thee."

MEDITATION *ALSO:*

STRENGTHENS FAITH

Psalm 104:33-34 "I will sing unto the LORD as long as I live: I will sing praise to my God while I have my being. My meditation of Him shall be sweet: I will be glad in the LORD."

EASES THE MIND OF FEARFUL THOUGHTS

Psalm 119:147-148 "I rise before dawn and cry for help; I have put my hope in your word. My eyes stay open through the watches of the night, that I may meditate on your promises." New International Version

PROVIDES INSIGHT AND WISDOM

Psalm 119:99 "I have more understanding than all my teachers: for thy testimonies *are* my meditation."

GIVES US SUCCESS

Joshua 1:8 "This book of the law shall not depart out of thy mouth; but thou shalt meditate therein day and night, that thou mayest observe to do according to all that is written therein: for then thou shalt make thy way prosperous, and then thou shalt have good success."

Chapter Eleven
When You Pray... Pray Like This

TYPES OF PRAYERS

PRIVATE PRAYERS

Matthew 6:6 "But thou, when thou prayest, enter into thy closet, and when thou hast shut thy door, pray to thy Father which is in secret; and thy Father which seeth in secret shall reward thee openly."

EARLY MORNING – as the first thing we do before we become busy and distracted.

Mark 1:35 "And in the morning, rising up a great while before day, he went out, and departed into a solitary place, and there prayed."

EVENING PRAYER

Mark 6:46-47 "And when He had sent them away, He departed into a mountain to pray."

IN SOLITUDE – alone and away from other people in a quiet place.

Luke 5:16 "And He withdrew Himself into the wilderness, and prayed."

ALL NIGHT – a period of time devoted to prayer between evening and sunrise.

Luke 6:12 "And it came to pass in those days, that He went out into a mountain to pray, and continued all night in prayer to God."

WITH VERY CLOSE RELATIONSHIPS – people who are spiritual and sincere, who will agree with your prayers and who will keep your confidence.

Luke 9:18 "And it came to pass about an eight days after these sayings, He took Peter and John and James, and went up into a mountain to pray."

PRAYER POSTURES AND VOICES

Posture in prayer visualizes the inward reverence and spirituality of our hearts when we pray. Posture also expresses the need or type of prayer being prayed. For example; laying prostrate on the floor can suggest desperation, bowing may be done as a sign of reverence or standing would be the posture when praying with a group.

Whether laying down, standing, bowing or lifting hands, know that your heavenly Father will be attentive to your prayers.

KNEELING

Psalm 95:6 "O come, let us worship and bow down: let us kneel before the LORD our maker."

Daniel 6:10 "Now when Daniel knew that the writing was signed, he went into his house; and his windows being open in his chamber toward Jerusalem, he kneeled upon his knees three times a day, and prayed, and gave thanks before his God, as he did aforetime."

Luke 22:41 "And he was withdrawn from them about a stone's cast, and kneeled down, and prayed."

STANDING

1st Kings 8:22- 23 "And Solomon stood before the altar of the LORD in the presence of all the congregation of Israel, and spread forth his hands toward heaven: And he said, LORD God of Israel, *there is* no God like thee, in heaven above, or on earth beneath, who keepest covenant and mercy with thy servants that walk before thee with all their heart."

BOWING

Exodus 4:31 "And the people believed: and when they heard that the LORD had visited the children of Israel, and that he had looked upon their affliction, then they bowed their heads and worshipped."

LAYING DOWN

Matthew 26:39 "And he went a little further, and fell on his face, and prayed, saying, O my Father, if it be possible, let this cup pass from me: nevertheless not as I will, but as thou wilt."

UPLIFTED HANDS

Psalm 141:2 "Let my prayer be set forth before thee *as* incense; *and* the lifting up of my hands *as* the evening sacrifice."

SILENTLY

Psalm 5:1 "To the chief Musician upon Nehiloth, A Psalm of David. 'Give ear to my words, O LORD, consider my meditation."

WEEPING

Ezra 10:1 "Now when Ezra had prayed, and when he had confessed, weeping and casting himself down before the house of God, there assembled unto him out of Israel a very great congregation of men and women and children: for the people wept very sore."

IN A LOUD VOICE

Psalm 39:3 "The more I thought about it, the hotter I got, igniting a fire of words." New Living Translation

WITHOUT SOUND

1ˢᵗ Samuel 1:13 "For Hannah's prayer came from her heart, and though her lips were moving she made no sound: so it seemed to Eli that she was overcome with wine."

A SONG

Psalm 42:8 "But each day the LORD pours His unfailing love upon me, and through each night I sing His songs, praying to God who gives me life." New Living Translation

CRYING OUT TO GOD

This is a desperate prayer that may include weeping, shouting, yelling, pleading for a resolution to a personal issue or on behalf of someone else. It is a prayer that comes from the depths of a grieving and sorrowful soul. For example, David praying for restoration after he sinned with Bathsheba.

Psalm 51:10-12 "Create in me a clean heart, O God; and renew a right spirit within me. Cast me not away from thy presence; and take not thy holy spirit from me. Restore unto me the joy of thy salvation; and uphold me *with thy* free spirit.

A BLESSING – Jacob

Genesis 32:26 "And he said, Let me go, for the day breaketh. And he said, 'I will not let thee go, except thou bless me.'"

IN INTERCESSION – Moses

Exodus 32:31-32 "And Moses returned unto the LORD, and said, Oh, this people have sinned a great sin, and have made them gods of gold. Yet now, if thou wilt forgive their sins; and if not, blot me, I pray thee, out of thy book which thou hast written."

FOR WISDOM – Solomon

1ˢᵗ Kings 3:7-9 "Now, O LORD my God, You have made Your servant king in place of my father David, yet I am but a little child; I do not know how to go out or come in. Your servant is in the midst of Your people which You have chosen, a great people who are too many to be numbered or counted. So give Your servant an understanding heart to judge Your people to discern between good and evil. For who is able to judge this great people of Yours?" New American Standard Bible

IN NEED OF CLEANSING – David

Psalm 51:1-2 "To the chief Musician, A Psalm of David, when Nathan the prophet came unto him, after he had gone in to Bathsheba. Have mercy upon me, O God, according to thy loving-kindness: according unto the multitude of thy tender mercies blot out my transgressions. Wash me thoroughly from mine iniquity, and cleanse me from my sin."

PLEA FOR DELIVERANCE – Paul

2ⁿᵈ Corinthians 12:8-9 "Three times I pleaded with the Lord to take it away from me. But he said to me, "My grace is sufficient for you, for my power is made perfect in weakness." Therefore I will boast all the more gladly about my weaknesses, so that Christ's power may rest on me." New International Version

A DYING SOUL – The Penitent Thief

Luke 23:42 "And he said unto Jesus, Lord, remember me when thou comest into thy kingdom."

SALVATION – The Philippian Jailer

Acts 16:29-30 "Then the jailer called for lights, rushed in, and fell down trembling before Paul and Silas. And brought them out, and said, Sirs, what must I do to be saved?"

CAST ALL YOUR CONCERNS

Casting your cares is a practice we are encouraged to do in Scripture because it gives us peace of mind, settles our souls and strengthens our spirits as we pray during a trial. It means to throw, toss or fling something out of frustration or determination to be rid of its pressure. However, casting is more easily said than done because cares and concerns seem to have a way of boomeranging.

But because of God's love, having Jesus as our High Priest in Heaven interceding on our behalf and being guided by the Holy Spirit, casting is obtainable if we *practice:*

- ENCOURAGING OURSELVES – Speaking words, singing songs and reading scripture for encouragement.

- OCCUPYING OUR MINDS WITH SCRIPTURE – Because worry tends to sneak up in the night and interrupt our sleep we

60

should pray and read our Bible before bedtime.

- SETTING GOALS – Spending time working on a project brings fulfillment. It will also fill the space of "empty thoughts" in our minds with purpose.

- EXERCISING AND DIET – Exercise and healthy eating is not only good for our bodies, it stimulates our minds with inspiration and gives us a positive outlook on life.

- AVOIDANCE – Try to avoid negative and worrisome people because they have a way of unintentionally reigniting anxiety which aids the boomerang effect.

PRAY GOD'S WORD

The more truth is heard the more convinced and swayed we become by it. God's Word is the truth we believe will stabilize our lives; therefore, the more we hear it, the more we believe it. This is why we should quote the Scriptures when we pray. Praying Scriptures and making them declarations over our lives makes us stronger, brings satisfaction to our souls, increases our trust in God, and helps us to visualize His promises.

Roman 10:17 "So then faith *cometh* by hearing, and hearing by the word of God."

PRAY SPECIFICALLY

We've learned that our heavenly Father wants us to ask Him for the things that we need which should encourage us to be specific when we pray. There is no reason to shy away from His love and desire to answer our prayers.

1st Samuel 1:27 "For this child I prayed; and the LORD hath given me my petition which I asked of Him."

Zechariah 10:1 "Ask the LORD for rain in the springtime; it is the LORD who sends the thunderstorms. He gives showers of rain to all people, and plants of the field to everyone." New International Version

Matthew 7:8 "For every one that asketh receiveth; and he that seeketh findeth; and to him that knocketh it shall be opened."

Matthew 21:22 "And all things, whatsoever ye shall ask in prayer, believing, ye shall receive."

[1,2,3,4] From the devotional "The Secret Place of the Most High … How to Get There" © 2014 by Dr. Sheila Walker; S. Walker Publications, Altamonte Springs, FL 32716; www.swalkerpublications

21 DAY PRAYER JOURNAL

INSTRUCTIONS FOR YOUR 21 DAYS OF PRAYER JOURNEY

1. *Start your prayer with worship and praise to the Father*

2. *Select a quiet place at a specific time of day to pray*

3. *Include the Prayer Focus for each day to your prayer*

4. *Journal how your feelings and prayer improvement for each Prayer Focus*

5. *End your prayer with thanks in the Name of Jesus*

DAY 1 – PRAYER FOCUS: *Fervor (indifference)*
SCRIPTURE: *Isaiah 32:9*

DAY 2 – PRAYER FOCUS: *Instability*
SCRIPTURE: *James 1:6-7*

_____

_____

_____

_____

_____

_____

_____

_____

_____

_____

_____

_____

_____

_____

_____

_____

_____

_____

_____

_____

_____

_____

_____

_____

_____

_____

_____

DAY 3 – PRAYER FOCUS: *Self-indulgence*
SCRIPTURE: *James 4:3*

DAY 4 – PRAYER FOCUS: *Increased Sincerity*
SCRIPTURE: *Hebrews 10:22*

DAY 5 – PRAYER FOCUS: *Noticing Repetition*
SCRIPTURE: *Matthew 6:7*

_____

_____

_____

_____

_____

_____

_____

_____

_____

_____

_____

_____

_____

_____

_____

_____

_____

_____

_____

_____

_____

_____

_____

_____

_____

_____

DAY 6 – PRAYER FOCUS: *Confession and Contriteness*
SCRIPTURE: *1ˢᵗ John 1:9*

_____

_____

_____

_____

_____

_____

_____

_____

_____

_____

_____

_____

_____

_____

_____

_____

_____

_____

_____

_____

_____

_____

_____

_____

_____

DAY 7 – PRAYER FOCUS: *Forgiveness*
SCRIPTURE: *Ephesians 1:7*

DAY 8 – PRAYER FOCUS: *Forgiveness of Others*
SCRIPTURE: *Matthew 6:15*

DAY 9 – PRAYER FOCUS: *Worship in Prayer*
SCRIPTURE: *Psalm 95:2*

_____

_____

_____

_____

_____

_____

_____

_____

_____

_____

_____

_____

_____

_____

_____

_____

_____

_____

_____

_____

_____

_____

_____

DAY 10 – PRAYER FOCUS: *Meditation*
SCRIPTURE: *Psalm 77:12*

DAY 11 – PRAYER FOCUS: *Wisdom and Clarity*
SCRIPTURE: *James 1:5*

_____

_____

_____

_____

_____

_____

_____

_____

_____

_____

_____

_____

_____

_____

_____

_____

_____

_____

_____

_____

_____

_____

DAY 12 – PRAYER FOCUS: *Prayer for God's Will to be done*
SCRIPTURE: *Matthew 26:39*

DAY 13 – PRAYER FOCUS: *Patience while Waiting on God*
SCRIPTURE: *Isaiah 40:31*

DAY 14 – PRAYER FOCUS: *Worriedness, fearful thoughts or anxiety*
SCRIPTURE: *Philippians 4:6*

DAY 15 – PRAYER FOCUS: *Victory of Temptation*
SCRIPTURE: *James 4:7*

_____

_____

_____

_____

_____

_____

_____

_____

_____

_____

_____

_____

_____

_____

_____

_____

_____

_____

_____

_____

_____

_____

_____

_____

DAY 16 – PRAYER FOCUS: *Faith and Peace*
SCRIPTURE: *Luke 24:36*

DAY 17– PRAYER FOCUS: *Acknowledgement of God's Authority*
SCRIPTURE: *Matthew 6:9*

_____

_____

_____

_____

_____

_____

_____

_____

_____

_____

_____

_____

_____

_____

_____

_____

_____

_____

_____

_____

_____

_____

_____

_____

_____

DAY 18– PRAYER FOCUS: *Unity in Prayer for Others*
SCRIPTURE: *Matthew 18:19-20*

_____

_____

_____

_____

_____

_____

_____

_____

_____

_____

_____

_____

_____

_____

_____

_____

_____

_____

_____

_____

_____

_____

_____

DAY 19 – PRAYER FOCUS: *The Guidance of The Holy Spirit*
SCRIPTURE: *Romans 8:26*

DAY 20 – PRAYER FOCUS: *Recital of God's promises*
SCRIPTURE: *Romans 10:17*

_____

_____

_____

_____

_____

_____

_____

_____

_____

_____

_____

_____

_____

_____

_____

_____

_____

_____

_____

_____

_____

_____

_____

DAY 21 – PRAYER FOCUS: *Thankfulness*
SCRIPTURE: *Psalm 107:1*

_____

_____

_____

_____

_____

_____

_____

_____

_____

_____

_____

_____

_____

_____

_____

_____

_____

_____

_____

_____

_____

_____

_____

_____

_____

"And Jesus lifted up *his* eyes, and said, Father,
I thank thee that thou hast heard me."
John 11:41

Visit www.yourspirituallife.org for spiritual life coaching, free downloads, inspirational Bible Studies and discussions.

Also Available in this Study Devotional Series to empower your spiritual life further:

THE SECRET PLACE OF THE MOST HIGH ... HOW TO GET THERE
A self-help devotional with "Power Scriptures" to assist and guide you through difficult times in your life

FROM GLORY TO GLORY ... CHANGE AND TRANSITION
A study devotional that explains change and transition to help you fulfill your destiny

To Learn More about the Bible order:

THE INTRODUCTION SERIES:

Introduction to Bible Doctrine
A Systematic Study of Seven Doctrines of the Christian Faith – Made Easy

Introduction to Bible Origin
A Study of the Formation of the Bible

Introduction to Typology and Symbolism
An Expository Study of Types and Symbols Found in the Bible

To Receive a Certificate in Biblical Studies in five short months:
Go to: *www.theinstituteoftheology.org*

www.ingramcontent.com/pod-product-compliance
Lightning Source LLC
Chambersburg PA
CBHW062017040426
42447CB00010B/2035